At David C Cook, we equip the local church around the corner and around the globe to make disciples. Come see how we are working together—go to **www.davidccook.org**. Thank you!

DAVID C COOK

*transforming lives together*

What people are saying about …

# DONE WITH THAT

"In *Done with That*, Bob Merritt shows that less means more. Less regret means more joy. Less loneliness means more belonging. Less angst means more contentment. Bob's hard-fought battle will help you win yours."

—**Mark Batterson**, *New York Times*
bestselling author of *The Circle Maker*; lead
pastor, National Community Church

"Freedom in Christ is one of the most powerful gifts of the gospel. But knowledge of that freedom and walking in that freedom are two different things. This book moves us from knowledge to action, with practical application for every person who is truly ready to move. Thank you, Bob, for living that out in your own life and showing us the way for ourselves."

—**Kyle Idleman**, senior pastor, Southeast Christian
Church; author of *Not a Fan* and *The End of Me*

"How do you stop putting up with what you know you need to be done with? Bob Merritt has written an open, honest personal account about moving forward with God."

—**John Ortberg**, senior pastor, Menlo
Church; author of *Eternity Is Now in Session*

"People *talk* a lot about change these days, but here's the truth. No one ever really changes until it gets too painful to stay where they are. In other words, they have to get sick and tired of being sick and tired! If that's where you are, then Pastor Bob Merritt's *Done with That* is absolutely the book for you. It's a great prescription for turning your life around and reviving your walk with God."

—**Dave Ramsey**, bestselling author;
nationally syndicated radio show host

"In *Done with That*, Bob Merritt shares firsthand how exhausting it can be to endure the crushing weight of persistent problems. More importantly, though, he also knows the power we have through Jesus Christ to be more than conquerors! If you've ever struggled to stop fighting the same old battles so you can start living in Christ's victory, then *Done with That* is for you."

—**Chris Hodges**, senior pastor,
Church of the Highlands; author of
*The Daniel Dilemma* and *What's Next?*

"I found *Done with That* to be incredibly helpful. While Bob has plenty of success, he also has a fair amount of personal failure which he generously shares. He has a track record of saying, 'I'm done with that.' This is something I need to say more since spiritual growth includes leaving things behind. This is a great resource for the average person who wants an above average life."

—**Brian Tome**, senior pastor,
Crossroads Church; author of
*Five Marks of a Man* and *Free Book*

"*Done with That* is authentic, refreshing, and compelling! I loved how Bob Merritt's mix of humility and truth hits the mark and the heart. I read a lot of books and this one was just what I needed. Now, I am inspired to be done with some things so I can be and do even greater things."

—**David Horsager**, CEO, Trust Edge
Leadership Institute; bestselling author

"Your future is shaped by how well you lead yourself. And there is nobody better than Bob Merritt to show how to lead yourself well. *Done with That* brilliantly looks at how you can let go of the past and embrace a better future. Read it, live it, and share it."

—**Jud Wilhite**, author of *Pursued*;
senior pastor of Central Church

"*Done with That* is an honest book. I was drawn in by Merritt's refreshing vulnerability and the absence of 'spiritual fluff.' These pages offer hope and grace for maturing leaders. Candid. Funny. Convicting."

—**Jeff Manion**, senior pastor, Ada Bible Church; author
of *Dream Big, Think Small* and *The Land Between*

"A master storyteller, Bob opens his life to the reader, letting you experience his own failures. He leads you through a process of change and shows the path to a hope-filled future. With heart and humor, Bob brilliantly speaks to a challenge everyone has, and ultimately provides the tools to be done with that."

—**Dean Hager**, CEO, Jamf

"A gifted storyteller, Bob Merritt writes with grace, self-awareness, and vulnerability. His genuine honesty about his struggles not only challenges us to a new life when tempted to fall back into old patterns but gives us hope."

—**Deb Schoneman**, president,
Piper Jaffray Companies

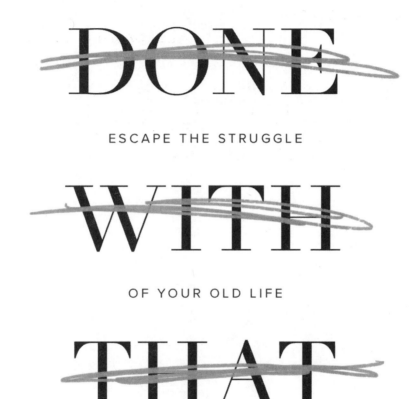

# DONE

ESCAPE THE STRUGGLE

# WITH

OF YOUR OLD LIFE

# THAT

BOB MERRITT

DAVID C COOK

*transforming lives together*

*To Laurie*
*I thank God every day for the gift you are to me.*
*For forty years now, imperfect together.*

DONE WITH THAT
Published by David C Cook
4050 Lee Vance Drive
Colorado Springs, CO 80918 U.S.A.

Integrity Music Limited, a Division of David C Cook
Brighton, East Sussex BN1 2RE, England

The graphic circle C logo is a registered trademark of David C Cook.

The website addresses recommended throughout this book are offered as a
resource to you. These websites are not intended in any way to be or imply an
endorsement on the part of David C Cook, nor do we vouch for their content.

Unless otherwise noted, all Scripture quotations are taken from THE HOLY
BIBLE, NEW INTERNATIONAL VERSION®, NIV® Copyright © 1973, 1978,
1984, 2011 by Biblica, Inc.® Used by permission. All rights reserved worldwide.
Scripture quotations marked NCV are taken from the New Century Version®.
Copyright © 2005 by Thomas Nelson. Used by permission. All rights reserved;
NLT are taken from the *Holy Bible*, New Living Translation, copyright © 1996,
2007 by Tyndale House Foundation. Used by permission of Tyndale House
Publishers, Inc., Carol Stream, Illinois 60188. All rights reserved; NLV are taken
from the Holy Bible, New Life Version. Copyright © 1969–2003 by Christian
Literature International, P.O. Box 777, Canby, OR 97013. Used by permission.
The author has added italics to Scripture quotations for emphasis.

LCCN 2019930497
ISBN 978-0-8307-7710-5
eISBN 978-0-8307-7711-2

© 2019 Robert A. Merritt
Published in association with Don Gates at The Gates Group—www.gatesliterary.com.

The Team: Alice Crider, Megan Stengel, Rachael
Stevenson, Diane Gardner, Susan Murdock
Cover Design: Nick Lee

Printed in the United States of America
First Edition 2019

1 2 3 4 5 6 7 8 9 10

060719

# CONTENTS

# ACKNOWLEDGMENTS

Writing a book is a four-year process for me that starts with a stir, turns into a storm, becomes such a foreboding tempest that if I don't get it out, I can't sleep. I don't just decide to write a book. I'm essentially dragged into it by God's Spirit. If I were not convinced that God was behind it, I would never subject myself to the terror of the empty page or deep insecurities writing produces in me. I brought my best thinking, dreaming, and praying to these pages, but that's never enough. I look back on a few chapters I wrote four years ago and wonder, *Where did that come from?* Truly, from God's precious Holy Spirit. It's because of Him that anything good comes out of me, and it's to Him that I owe my most humble thanks.

So I get dragged into it, but then others get dragged into it with me. Thanks to Don Gates (The Gates Group), who believed in this project from the jump. Deep gratitude to Alice Crider, Rachael Stevenson, Nathan Landry, Nick Lee, and all the others at David C Cook—you've treated me like one of your own.

Huge thanks to Heidi Anderson and Kristin Sanford for your creative touches. I'm indebted to Shannon Schmidt, Karianne Langfield, T. J. Therrien, Travis Wermedal, and John Alexander for your ongoing help and support.

To my dearest mom, Barb Merritt, now eighty-seven years old, your daily prayer for me is what fuels my life. I owe so much of who I am to you and Dad, who showed me what it means to trust Jesus daily.

To my church, Eagle Brook—look what God has done. Simply amazing.

Most of all, thanks to Laurie, Meg, Dave, Nelly, and Sara. You are the five most important people to me on the planet. There aren't words to describe how much I love you. I hit the lottery.

# STRUGGLING TO LEAVE

"I'm done with that!"

When was the last time you said those words? Maybe you were fed up with a job going nowhere. Perhaps you had a habit that kept embarrassing you or a past failure that haunted you. Whatever the issue was, a point came when you threw up your hands and in exasperation cried, "I'm done with that!"

There's power in saying that.

When our second child was on the way, the timing was bad. I was pastoring a small country church in Falun, Wisconsin, but after five years of isolation and low pay ($12,000 a year), I wondered whether I still wanted to be a pastor. We had no money and all our earthly belongings crammed into a small U-Haul trailer that we pulled behind our junky 1969 Cutlass Supreme. That was when we decided I'd return to school and enroll in the speech program at Penn State University. We were going from poor to very poor with no permanent job in sight for at least another three years. And to top it all off, Laurie was seven months pregnant.

I must confess: I'm not much of a baby person. Some people go gaga over babies. Not me. Don't get me wrong; every baby is a miraculous gift from God. But all the crying, clinging, sucking, spitting, wailing, and overall chaos? I'm not cut out for it.

I quickly realized this with our first. And by the time news came of our second, I felt in way over my head. Candidly, I didn't know whether I could handle another round of sleepless nights, marital tension, and sour spit-up.

But that's exactly the situation I faced. With a toddler in tow, a baby on the way, a move, and a return to school, I thought, *That's it. We're done. I'm done.* So when the time came for Laurie and me to decide whether we'd have more children, I didn't vacillate. There was a vasectomy but no vacillating. After two kids we were done. And we never looked back.

What are you done with?

Here's a common answer: money problems—patterns of overspending, borrowing against credit cards … Have you been there? You just want to be done with it? The good news is you can. And the way you do that with finances illustrates many of the truths this book explores, principles that apply to almost any change we desire in our lives.

Five years ago I made a verbal declaration regarding finances to the twenty-four thousand people who attend our services. At the time, our church carried a large debt of $18 million on our first campus, and for twenty years we'd been paying it down in small increments. It was so tiring. Whenever we wanted to expand our reach, we contended with our debt, and it became an albatross around our necks. We couldn't build other campuses, though we sensed God leading that way, and couldn't pay our staff as we should have. Then we made the mistake of borrowing more—debt on top of debt! Everything in my being railed against it, but I allowed the pursuit of our mission to trump our ability to pay for it.

Eventually I became so burdened and convicted by this I said, "No more." I actually asked myself, *Merritt, who's holding the gun to your head? You're the senior pastor. What are* you *going to do about it?*

That was a defining moment for me. From that moment on, I declared, "No more debt! We are done with that!" I informed our staff, board, and church. I repeated it and continue to repeat it. I said, "Where's the faith in taking out a loan? Let's challenge ourselves, trust God, and raise the money! If we fall short, we won't build until we have the money."

Five diligent years later, our church is nearly debt free, and we pay for our new campuses and expansions in cash. It all started with a single declaration: "We are done with that!"

Do you need to be done with something that's hurting you, preventing you from achieving your dreams, or hindering God's call on your life? It might be mental, financial, spiritual, or even relational.

Perhaps you need to be done with a certain person. That might seem harsh, but it's true. You might have an abusive, alcoholic, or intensely manipulative parent, and after years of seeing no change, you need to be done with that. Nobody wins in that situation, but if that person refuses to change his or her behavior, you can at least govern your own and establish some new boundaries.

Maybe it's not a parent; it could be an irresponsible sibling, so you're the one who picks up after his or her messes. You rescue her kids, bail him out financially, or serve as her emotional dumping zone. Who's that helping? Certainly not your irresponsible family member. As long as that sibling knows you're there to pick him or her up, your brother or sister will never shape up. Because, well, why would he? Why should she? And it's certainly not helping you. You resent it, live with anger, and then feel guilty when you call him or her on it. Stop feeling guilty.

Be done with that. All of it! You can pray for your loved ones and offer your kindness, but you have to stop enabling their dysfunction and irresponsible lifestyles.

You and I will encounter people at work, at school, and in our communities who refuse to take responsibility for their lives. Pray for them, offer wisdom and support if you can, but then know where the line is. A time comes when you have to say, "That's hurtful, that's wrong, that's not good for you or me—so I'm done; we're done." It's really about being able to say no. For every wise no, there's a better yes.

- No to lying, yes to trusting.
- No to manipulating, yes to relating.
- No to taking, yes to sharing.
- No to isolation, yes to connecting.
- No to debt, yes to financial freedom.
- No to sexual misconduct, yes to relational integrity.
- No to anger, yes to inner peace.
- No to addiction, yes to sobriety.

Here's the problem. There are things about you I don't like and things about me you don't like. And in spite of His love for us, there are things about all of us God dislikes because of what they do to us.

I'm a fellow struggler with you. All my life I've heard preachers say if you put your trust in Jesus, "the old [life] has gone, the new [life] is here" (2 Cor. 5:17). Then why do I still snap at my wife sometimes? Why do I still say words I regret? Why do I still get angry, struggle with greed, and battle nagging insecurities? If the old life is gone and a new life has come, why do I repeat habits I know hurt myself and others? These questions bother me, and I've struggled with them most of my life. But it must be possible to be done with the old life, or the Bible wouldn't have said it is possible. So how? And is it really worth the effort?

I never write a book just to write a book. I'm pulled into it kicking and screaming. I don't need the moments of terror when I think I don't have one new thing to contribute to society. But when God grabs my spirit and convicts me of something bothersome and compelling, I know I have to get it out or I'm going to explode. Jesus came to give us life to the full (see John 10:10)—not for us to be enslaved by sin or doomed to failure. A full, free life. I don't know about you, but that's what I want. I'm ready to be done with the chains of that old life, and I'm ready to press into the new. I'm honored to have you join the adventure with me.

PART I

# GETTING HONEST

# WHAT I NEVER KNEW ABOUT THE NEW LIFE

In 2004 I reached a breaking point. Our church had grown from 350 people to over ten thousand in just twelve years. We were building buildings and adding staff; plus, the number of requests for me to teach and lead outside our church was increasing. On the outside, most would have considered us a thriving church and me a successful pastor, and by all accounts it looked that way.

But I was miserable.

The demands on my life exceeded my ability to keep up, and I was tethered to so many people and so many obligations that I felt suffocated. One day things finally caught up with me, and I needed out. Although rain poured outside, I took my canoe to a local lake and paddled out to the middle. Then with rain and tears streaming down my face, I looked up toward the sky and said out loud, "What's wrong with me?" I was emotionally and physically exhausted.

The cracks became evident through my harsh comments and bursts of anger. In the office I had become a virtual recluse, sequestered behind a closed door to crank out another sermon or news article. My staff rarely approached me or even had access to me, but when they did, the tension was thick—almost explosive. If someone got hurt or offended, so what? Nobody cared. Nobody had *time* to care.

It was even worse at home. I stormed around in anger, reacting to even the smallest things with hurtful jabs and unkind gestures. The kids learned to stay clear and quietly wondered to my wife, "What's wrong with Dad?" Between Laurie and me, there was plenty of yelling and tears, followed by days of the cold shoulder and staying out of each other's way.

But frankly, I was blind to my problems and didn't understand why I felt or reacted the way I did. I excused my behavior because I truly believed I was doing what God wanted. And that was true—I *was* doing what God had led me to do. Only I was doing too much of it. I was emotionally depleted and relationally dangerous, and I couldn't recall the last time I had laughed.

What I didn't know was that my church board was having serious behind-the-scenes conversations about my future. Until, at a board meeting one night, they told me I must get some professional help—or I was done.

I was so stunned I couldn't speak. Has something ever made you feel that way? Something surprising, something awful happened, and it shook you to the core? I realized that those eight people held my fate in their hands, and at that moment I had a choice—either I admitted and addressed some serious flaws, or I risked losing everything I'd given my life to.

That conversation launched a yearlong intervention with a guy named Fred, who specializes in executive coaching. Fred and his team took me through every self-evaluation assessment known to man. They interviewed all my family members, most of my staff, and all my closest friends using sixty questions that asked, "What's good about Bob, and what's bad about Bob?"

Those they interviewed held nothing back, and some even used the opportunity to thrust and twist the dagger in as deep as they could. At the end, every comment was recorded in a two-hundred-page document and read back to me by Fred and his assistant over a two-day lockdown.

Those were the most painful two days of my life.

It was also the first time I'd received any sort of in-depth professional insight into my behavior patterns. And I know now that it saved me.

I immediately resigned some of my commitments—the heaviest being a teaching role at Bethel Seminary—and soon I began seeing the connection between my stress and my anger. I had a long way to go, and the battle wouldn't be won immediately. But at least I was becoming more aware of my problems.

## SIGNS OF HOPE

I knew I had to live and lead differently, but I was also afraid I wouldn't be able to change. So I asked Fred how many guys like me grow and actually see transformation. He was honest: "About 40 percent. Those who succeed are humble. They not only receive the feedback but apply it to their lives." Well, if humility was the key to change, I would do my best to take all the feedback in—and pray for grace.

Over the next ten years, change became noticeable, especially in how I treated people. Some of my staff even said, "What's happened to Bob is a miracle." My stress was lower, and my anger was under control. Instead of just blurting out the first thing that came to mind, I actually thought about my words before I spoke. And rather than criticizing people, I sought ways to compliment them. I wasn't perfect, I still failed, but I saw my faults more quickly and owned up to them more willingly.

During those ten years, our church grew from ten thousand to twenty thousand attendees, the budget doubled, and we added four campuses, making a total of seven. None of that would have happened if I had only tried to tweak the dial and muddle through. I had to seek help, listen to my elders, follow Fred's advice, and, lastly but most importantly, humble myself before God.

The Bible says, "God opposes the proud but shows favor to the humble" (James 4:6). It's not that God simply puts up with the proud or is indifferent to their arrogance, but He actively *opposes* them. But to the humble? To those who are teachable and willing? He gives grace, forgiveness, and, thankfully for me, second chances.

## MORE CRACKS

So God gifted me with another chance, and our church enjoyed an amazing ten years. But then more cracks in my armor showed. Although I had genuinely improved in managing my stress, anger, and word choices, deeper, unexplored issues still wreaked havoc on our church staff. Pain signals that something is wrong. I was experiencing pain, particularly in the form of a couple of senior staff resignations and growing tension among the other staff. Candidly, I thought I could manage it. But the church board asked whether I'd be open to another round with Fred.

I responded calmly and willingly, but inside I thought, *You gotta be kidding me. Not Fred again. I thought I was done with that.*

What I learned is *you're never done with that.* It was a huge revelation to me—you're never done growing, never done learning, never done dealing with your weaknesses.

This time Fred dug deeper into my upbringing. He had me map out, starting from my childhood, all my life experiences—those that had a positive effect and those that had a negative impact. By doing this, I started seeing where my feelings of fear, insecurity, and lack of trust originated.

For example, I had loving parents, but when I was eight years old, they traveled to Argentina for a month and farmed us five kids out to different families. One night a blizzard hit the Chicago area where we lived, but I had 120 newspapers to deliver after school. The snow piled up to my thighs, each step was a battle, and completing the route took five hours. When I was done, I stumbled into my caretakers' garage after nine at night. I was cold and crying, and they *yelled* at me. They wondered where I was, and they had called the police.

I don't remember anything else about that night or even the whole month—except feeling completely abandoned and unloved.

Then as I looked back, I also remembered moving a lot. Not only did it make life feel unstable, but each new school I attended also made me feel more alone.

I never told anyone about these things—until I met with Fred.

After I made my list, Fred took me through an evaluation grid with four quadrants: integrity, responsibility, forgiveness, and compassion. Through seven years of extensive research, he had found that these four character qualities give a person a sense of wholeness.

To understand how I rated in these four areas, Fred sent my colleagues a questionnaire. When the results came back, I had strong scores in the areas of integrity and responsibility—but I completely failed in forgiveness and compassion. This raised a big red flag for Fred, but I kept thinking, *What do forgiveness and compassion have to do with leadership anyway?*

After that initial intervention, Fred coached me for eight more months and asked me strange questions like these:

"What was it about your dad and your upbringing that causes you to lack compassion for people today?"

*Huh?*

Or "Why are you so afraid to forgive yourself and others?"

*What?*

Or "When you discover the fuel for forgiveness, don't you think you'll be happier and freer?"

*Come again?*

I'd never heard questions like that and at first had no clue what they meant. Fred concluded that my lack of forgiveness and compassion was primarily fear driven, but I didn't understand that. He said my fear of failure contributed to my inability to forgive myself or others, but I didn't understand that either.

Fred pointed out how my dad modeled a lack of forgiveness and compassion. Now, I have to be clear—I loved my dad. He was faithful to my mom, family, and church, and he was a great leader. But he was pretty rigid and emotionless. He saw the world as black and white, so he had little patience for those who fell outside his framework. And come to think of it, he wasn't very forgiving of or compassionate toward himself or others either.

Turns out, the apple really doesn't fall far from the tree, because I struggle with those same things. Like my dad I'm unusually hard on myself and others. But I'm finding that to break free from the old life of fear and insecurity, I need to be more patient with those who think differently than me, and I have to be more forgiving. It'll involve letting myself and others fail and being okay with some of it.

This is not natural for me, and I can easily flip back into my previous rigid, judgmental, unforgiving mode. But I can sense a shift in my spirit as I practice letting myself and others off the hook, and it's a wonderful thing.

In his book *Unoffendable*, Brant Hansen wrote, "Quit thinking it's up to you to police people.... Quit trying to parent the whole world.... Quit being shocked when people don't share your morality. Quit serving as judge and jury.... *It's all so exhausting.*"[1]

I'm starting to get that. He wasn't saying that we shouldn't care about right and wrong but that we don't have to be so forceful with it all the time.

I still speak up when I think a staff member is wrong, and I still get upset when someone makes a decision I don't agree with. I still tell the truth and hold people accountable. That's part of being a good leader, a good person.

But now I'm working to slow down and take a more thoughtful approach. I ask more questions instead of making blanket statements. I try not to weigh in on every little decision as if my life depends on it. And I've committed to linking arms with my executive pastor more—to trust him and others to represent my heart and execute our plans and vision. At one time I gave people directives and then scurried around the office ensuring they talked to the right people and did everything exactly as instructed. But now? I'm done with that.

## WE HAVE MORE TIME THAN WE THINK

One of the most helpful insights I received during this time came from another Fred. Fred Martin, president of Disciplined Growth Investors, manages large investment accounts like government pension funds for entire states. He also leads a divorce care group at our church with his wife, Sue, and these two have become wonderful friends and mentors.

Recently Fred and I were on a two-hour drive from the airport to his Montana ranch, and I asked for his advice about a decision one of my colleagues had made recently. I was bothered by this person's choice and wanted to address it swiftly.

Fred listened intently and then said, "Bob, with most issues and decisions like this, you have a lot more time than you think."

*Huh?*

He waved his hands, barely able to get the words out fast enough: "If we see something we don't like or we see someone making a bad decision, we often think, *I have to go fix that right now.* We immediately shoot off an email, approach that person, and try to fix the problem *right that very moment.*"

Fred looked at me and said, "Stop doing that. Do you need to call that person right now? Or is there a better time—like when you have more information? Do you have to insert yourself into every decision, or can you let other people make choices, allowing *them* to feel the satisfaction when they're right … and the pain when they're wrong?"

I had never thought of that.

I decided to take Fred's advice. I wish I could report it was easy and freeing; it wasn't. I struggled to let the matter go and not let it bother me, but I kept thinking I should pick up the phone and make sure my colleague understood my disappointment. But I finally *did* let it go. I decided I had more time than I thought, so I surrendered the issue to God, enjoyed the week hunting elk in Montana, and then eased my way into the matter when I returned home. The issue was resolved, nobody drew blood, trust was built, and I discovered that *I have a lot more time than I think*. The Bible advises, "Be … slow to speak and slow to become angry" (James 1:19). Slow it down. Take a walk. Step away and get some perspective. You can still come back and say what you were going to say originally. But I've found it's worth exploring whether there's a better time, place, or way to resolve the issue first.

## MORE SIGNS OF GROWTH

I'm kind of a water Nazi. I don't like leaky faucets, and I don't like overflushing—so flushing bugs down the toilet is out of the question. I also think the dishwasher should be jam-packed before we run it, because there's no need to waste even a drop of water. So when my wife was on the phone the other day and failed to shut off the faucet precisely when the water reached the top of the slow cooker she was preparing to soak, I felt an urge to reach over, shut it off, and give her a condescending look. But I thought, *Give her a second. Don't be a jerk. See if you can refrain from being the correction officer.*

And guess what? She reached over and turned it off (three seconds too late in my mind, but she did it). And she never knew how I felt or what I was thinking. She didn't need to know.

That's spiritual growth for me.

Seriously, it is.

Spiritual maturity often gets tested in the tiny things that pop up every day. These tests come in the form of little annoyances, such as an ill-timed comment that someone makes, a misplaced phone, overstuffed drawers, annoying quirks, or cupboard doors left open. Laurie knows this to be true—she says I leave a trail of open doors and closets every day that she has to close, and it tests her patience.

It's hard to let certain things go for the sake of relationships. And as you gain more responsibility as a parent, teacher, manager, author, builder, or leader, the tests get tougher and the need for self-control becomes greater.

But the alternative is to stay stuck. Keep offending. Never improve, and fail to achieve. Let's be done with that. You and I have to break out of the old life and into the new.

What follows are two realities I never knew until recently.

## YOU'RE NEVER DONE GROWING

I thought I had arrived after my first round with Fred—but then I learned you're never done growing, never done battling. On this side of heaven, we won't be able to say, "I made it, I'm a new person, and I never have to deal with sin again." In fact, the more you shine the light of God's truth on your "old life" patterns and sins, the more you see how much work still needs to be done.

It's like peeling an onion. Anger is my top layer, but strip that back, and you'll uncover a lack of forgiveness and compassion driving that anger. What are your layers? Peel one away, and there's another deeper, more hidden layer to deal with that maybe you never realized was there.

Some of you might say, "If the battle against sin is never done, then why even try? Why not just give up and indulge myself in whatever I desire? Why subject myself to the disciplines of counseling, reading, praying, self-constraint, repentance, and forgiveness when ultimate joy and wholeness are unattainable?"

In his book *The Spirit of the Disciplines*, Christian philosopher Dallas Willard addressed the challenge of living the Christian life. He said the word *disciple* appears 269 times in the New Testament but the word *Christian* appears only three times.[2] Why make that distinction? A disciple upholds disciplines. While others may see their regimen as burdensome or boring, these people faithfully maintain their disciplines out of dedication to Jesus. And as Christ taught, these disciplines provide the pathway to personal and relational wholeness.

Professional athletes know this well. They adhere to demanding disciplines and a boring regimen of drills, and they repeat them over and over again. Why? So they can defeat their opponents and experience the personal and professional fulfillment that comes with winning. If they neglect their daily disciplines, the result will be the exact opposite—personal, financial, and professional loss. It's no different with the Christian life. Willard wrote, "There is almost universal belief in the immense difficulty of being a *real* Christian. The vast, grim 'cost of discipleship' is something we hear constantly emphasized.... But it must not be left to stand as the whole truth. We would do far better to lay a clear, constant emphasis upon the cost of *non*-discipleship as well."[3]

The battle to overcome my sinful patterns isn't easy, and I'm profoundly disappointed when the things I've worked so hard to overcome resurface in the form of sharp words, flashes of anger, self-centeredness, or a lack of compassion. But although the battle is relentless, I'm gaining ground.

I'm not *as* angry, *as* self-centered, or *as* hard on others as I used to be. Before, I couldn't get through a single day without some kind of relational angst or flare-up, but now I enjoy longer stretches of relational peace. I'm more confident in my strengths and more accepting of my deficits. I feel genuinely content with my life and with those who are in my life. And in recent years, my relationship with God has changed from being rather distant and forced to being that of a son who enjoys walking through every day with his kind, benevolent, and proud Father.

The cost of discipleship is real, but the price of non-discipleship is a life that never improves and stays stuck in relational breakdown and personal strife. I thought I was done with that, but you're never really done with that.

## THERE ARE STAGES OF GROWTH

I had no idea that the deeper layers of the onion, the issues that are harder to detect, actually fueled the more obvious ones. My lack of forgiveness and compassion was causing some of my anger and harsh words.

When you can't forgive yourself for making a mistake, you're hard on yourself. When you're hard on yourself, you're hard on others. When you're hard on others, you lack compassion for them.

I thought that if I managed my anger and my mouth, I would nail it. I thought those were my signature sins and, if I could control those, then I was pretty close to being perfect. Our church's success over the previous ten years fooled me into thinking I had spiritually arrived.

However, when the cracks reappeared and Fred reentered the picture, I received another 125 pages of "fun" feedback.

That's the nature of spiritual growth. It comes in stages and waves. Overcome one thing, and there's another. Get a handle on one problem, and there's sure to be something else hiding beneath, deeper still.

Yet even here God is gracious and patient. Not only does He understand what we're made of, but He also knows growth takes time. Babies don't walk right away; they roll around, crawl, then walk and run. Adults also experience growth in stages, and it's tough to progress to the next milestone until you've gained some awareness and control in the previous stage.

The other day Fred met with our team for one last go-around, and he kicked off the meeting by having everyone comment on the growth we've seen in one another. The conversation moved around the room until the spotlight landed on me. As I wrote down each of the comments, one of them really stuck out. A colleague looked at me from across the table and said, "Ten years ago you made some great changes in your behavior, and you began treating people much better. But now you actually really care about people, and it's genuine. I can feel it in your spirit, and others can too."

You'll never know how grateful I was to hear that. And it's true. I'm actually starting to like people! God wants our love to be sincere. Sadly, mine once wasn't.

For years I taught that love is primarily a behavior, not a feeling. And to some degree, that is true. Like when I choose to forgive someone, that's a loving action—not a feeling. When I'm patient with people or tell the truth about their sin, that's an act of love—once again, not feeling. Love is an action, whether I like the person or not. So for years I excused myself from trying to *like* people. I thought as long as I behaved lovingly toward them by being patient or telling them the truth, then I was good with God.

But then I read Romans 12:10: "Love each other with genuine affection" (NLT). In other words, don't just act in loving ways toward people—make an effort to like them too. I had no idea how to do that (and I still struggle with it). For me it goes back to learning how to forgive myself. To give grace when I fail and tone it down when I'm tempted to beat myself up. Because if I can't bury the hatchet with myself, how can I forgive or show compassion to others?

I'm slowly learning that when I extend forgiveness—to myself and others—my compassion grows. And as my compassion grows, I start to feel genuine affection for others too. I'm beginning to like people, and miracle of miracles, they're starting to like me back. And that feels so good.

It doesn't matter where you are or how far you've come; we're never done growing. What matters is that we're willing to keep getting better—because the cost of discipleship is real but the cost of non-discipleship is greater.

## DISCUSSION QUESTIONS

1. How do you handle feedback? Receiving it can make us better, so how can you actively seek it out and listen more effectively when it is given?

2. What little annoyances do you need to let go of for the sake of your relationships?

3. When have you felt as if you experienced victory, won the battle, and were done with something—only later to have it resurface? Explain what contributed to this happening. How could you have prevented that issue's return?

2

# WHY THE OLD LIFE WON'T DIE

When we trust in Jesus, "the old [life] has gone, the new [life] is here" (2 Cor. 5:17). This promised change sounds instantaneous. But that hasn't been my experience. If the old life is gone, why is it still challenging me? Why do I still struggle with sin? Why do I still get angry, petty, and afraid? The Bible commands, "Do not be anxious about anything" (Phil. 4:6), but I'm anxious about everything—my job, my kids, my money, even starting this book.

A couple of years ago, my wife and I drove to the Mayo Clinic in Rochester, Minnesota, to visit my daughter and son-in-law, who are both in residency there. Along the way I noticed several road construction projects on the north-bound side that would affect our drive home. I remember Laurie specifically saying, "Look at all the traffic going north; they're at a standstill." It was 10 a.m., though, so I confidently replied that it wouldn't be a problem by the time we headed back.

Fast-forward to our drive home, and we whisked through a construction zone with no traffic at all. So I said to my wife, "See? No problem." To which she responded, "But this wasn't the spot with all the traffic. It was closer to the Twin Cities."

Knowing she was wrong, I felt obliged to correct her. "No way. This is the spot. It was closer to Rochester—I'm sure of it."

She matched my intensity, saying, "No, this *isn't* the spot. It was closer to the cities. Just wait and see."

Now, a wiser and more measured man would've let it go. A more thoughtful man would've realized even if I *were* right (which I was), nothing would be gained by proving I was right. Instead, I said, "Not a chance. I'm absolutely positive this is the spot." I *knew* I was right and she was wrong. In fact, I was so sure of it, I added, "I'll bet a hundred dollars I'm right" (which was so stupid because she manages all our money anyway). "You heard right—I'll bet a hundred dollars this is the spot. I marked it in my memory."

I could tell I'd planted a seed of doubt in her mind and she was softening, which made me all the more sure.

She said, "I still think it's closer to the city."

"Nope, this is it." And then I added, "I can't believe you doubt me like that."

She shot back, "Are you kidding me? You're wrong about stuff like this all the time."

I said, "Yeah, but not this time."

And I *was* right, so right, so sure, so happy in my correctness … until about twenty miles south of the city. That was when I noticed an orange construction sign ahead, followed by some orange barrels, and a long line of traffic backed up for miles. I came to a complete stop, and I hoped Laurie wouldn't notice. But she *did* notice. She's generally a kind and forgiving person but not this time. She was boiling mad, so angry that it struck my funny bone, and I started laughing. Which made her even more irate.

And then it happened.

She called me a bad word.

She called me a donkey's rear end—only the real thing.

I said, "You're not allowed to call me that!"

She said, "Well, that's what you are!" And then under her breath, I heard her say, "Idiot." And I laughed until I cried.

After I wrote this story down, I called her at home and read it aloud, and we both laughed all over again. Early in our marriage, this little battle of the wills would've sent us into a tailspin. Even still, in the spirit of transparency, what happened in the car that day happens more often than I care to admit. And I'm a *pastor*. We get into a tangle, words fly, and one or both of us slink away into our own corner and think, *Why is that person such a jerk?* If I'm honest with myself, I have to admit, *Why am I such a donkey's behind?*

## COMMON TO ALL

I've been a Christian since I was five years old, totaling fifty-seven years. I pray and read the Bible every day, and I teach it to others for my job. But if you haven't figured it out by now, I still sin—sometimes embarrassingly. I get mad, say hurtful things, and punish people I love with the silent treatment. You wouldn't believe how long I can hang on to a grudge—to the point where I can freeze people out of my life. And in my darker moments, I envy those more successful than me (and am a little glad when they fail). Sin is ugly and hurtful.

Here's the thing: sin is *always* destructive in nature. That's one indication that a habit, thought, or behavior is sinful—it's sin if it's destructive to yourself and others, and it's sin if it damages relationships. You can see the difference in the way parents correct children with firm but gentle love instead of disciplining with anger or the way bosses appropriately reprimand subordinates with the intent to help them, rather than shaming or berating them. Sin harms. Sin destroys. Sin leaves a wake of pain.

And all of us sin. Even the pope—*the pope*. The day Pope Francis was installed, he confessed, "I am a sinner, but I trust in the infinite mercy and patience of our Lord Jesus Christ."[1] Refreshing, don't you think?

I've been around some really great men and women who pastor large churches, lead massive organizations, author books, and give to the poor—and all of them have the same problem I have. They all sin. They struggle with tensions in their marriages, conflicts with coworkers, nagging insecurities, sexual temptation, and selfishness.

The Bible says, "We all stumble in many ways" (James 3:2). That could be my life verse. I stumble in *many, many* ways, and sometimes I'm aware of this reality. But I'm more concerned when I'm not cognizant of where I'm stumbling and sinning.

C. S. Lewis had been an atheist and admittedly far from God's truth. But after he became a Christian, Lewis wrote about how people become aware of their blindness to sin:

> When a man is getting better he understands more
> and more clearly the evil that is still left in him.
> When a man is getting worse he understands his own
> badness less and less. A moderately bad man knows

he is not very good: a thoroughly bad man thinks he is all right. This is common sense, really. You understand sleep when you are awake, not while you are sleeping. You can see mistakes in arithmetic when your mind is working properly: while you are making them you cannot see them. You can understand the nature of drunkenness when you are sober, not when you are drunk. *Good people know about both good and evil: bad people do not know about either.*[2]

The closer you draw to God and His truth, the more aware of your sin you actually become. The more aware you become, the more you realize just how far from God you've been in the first place and how sinful you still are.

## WHAT'S GONE, THEN?

The Bible says, "The old [life] has gone" (2 Cor. 5:17). But we know that in some sense it hasn't. We still sin, and people who say otherwise forgot about the times they lost their temper with the kids, gossiped about friends behind their backs, or withheld forgiveness. Sins like these dance in our faces each day. So what did Paul mean when he said, "The old [life] has gone"?

What's actually gone?

First, being *separated* from God is gone. Ephesians 2:12 says, "At that time you were separate from Christ," but because of Jesus' work on the cross, that gap no longer exists. We now have direct access to God. And amazingly enough, Jesus calls us His brothers and sisters and God the Father's sons and daughters (see Eph. 1:5;

Heb. 2:11). Those are *family terms*, and in His unlimited grace, God has welcomed us into His family forever.

Second, *hopelessness* is gone. Before Jesus paid for our sins, we were "without hope and without God in the world" (Eph. 2:12). But now we have hope. Not the kind of hope that wonders whether something might happen, but the kind of confident hope that knows something *will* happen because of God's promise. Jesus assured us that our sins are forgiven, we're welcomed into God's family, and we have eternal life awaiting us when we die.

Third, the *penalty* for sin is gone. Jesus bore the full penalty for our sins—every past, present, and future sin—and paid for them once and for all with His life and death on the cross. Yes, we still commit sins, and when we do, consequences follow. Dishonesty leads to relational breakdown; anger leads to emotional turmoil; and overspending leads to financial enslavement. We still sin, but the eternal penalty for our sins? Gone.

Fourth, *bondage* to sin is gone. We all sin, but we don't have to be enslaved to it. Romans 6:6 says, "Our old self was crucified with [Jesus] so that the body ruled by sin might be done away with, that we should no longer be slaves to sin." We still make mistakes, we still fail, and we still give in to temptation. But when Jesus rose from the dead, He broke sin's stranglehold on us. So even though we're not totally free from sin's insidious pull on our lives, we aren't doomed to enslavement to it either.

And finally, *eternal death* is gone. "If we have been united with him in a death like his, we will certainly also be united with him in a resurrection like his" (Rom. 6:5). All of us will die physically, but those of us who are united with Jesus by faith will pass through physical death and enter eternal life in heaven forevermore.

So all of that's gone! We don't have to live another moment separated, hopeless, at risk of eternal punishment, in bondage, or in fear of eternal death. As soon as we put our faith in Christ, these realities of the old life have completely vanished. Now we can hold our heads high, knowing love, hope, forgiveness, freedom, and eternal life are ours for the taking.

## WHAT ISN'T GONE?

We all have a nature that's part of us, and for every human being on this earth, it's clear we're all naturally selfish, greedy, lustful, and vindictive—we were born that way.

This isn't popular opinion. In fact, society's prevailing belief is that we're basically good, but the Bible teaches we're all born bad (see Rom. 3:23; Eph. 2:3). If you have kids, you understand that. A month-old baby lies there completely vulnerable; she can't roll over, can't even feed herself. She'd die in hours if someone didn't care for her every need. Yet thirty-six months later, that little baby will place her hands on her hips, glare at her mother, and say, "Get out of my life!" We came out of the womb as willful, life-sucking little monsters (told you I wasn't a baby person), and that spirit carries on throughout adulthood.

Nobody had to show me how to sin; I came by it naturally. No one had to teach me how to shade the truth, angle for the best seats, get seething mad in traffic, punish someone I love with the silent treatment, withhold affection, or steal a look for a little jolt of sexual gratification. Those things come easily to us because we have a nature that can lie dormant for weeks—but when triggered by the right stimulus, it can overwhelm any amount of resistance or good judgment we have.

Four years ago our beloved Chesapeake died, and we began the search for another dog. We found a reputable breeder of chocolate Labs in northern Minnesota, and with three males in the litter, my wife locked on to the biggest, most adorable chocolate we'd ever seen. The attachment was immediate, but the most important question remained: Could he hunt?

You should've heard Laurie. "Bob, look at him! He's the one."

I said, "We gotta give 'em the wing test." (For all you nonhunters, the wing test is when you take a pheasant wing and see how a dog reacts to it.)

We took him out into the grass, waved the pheasant wing in front of him, and tossed it a few feet away. He moseyed over, sniffed at it, and walked away. Laurie said, "Try it again," but this time that dog just lay down. I put him back in the pen and brought out dog number two. He showed a little more interest—sniffed the wing, picked it up, and then dropped it and walked away. Put him back in the pen too.

We'd already eliminated dog number three after the scrawny guy fell into the water dish, but when I waved the wing in front of him, he *lunged* for it. I tossed it out a few feet, and he *pounced* on it, then brought it right back to me.

Laurie held him back while I dragged the wing through the grass thirty feet away and hid it in some bushes. She let him go, and with his nose glued to the ground, he tracked that wing like a heat-seeking missile, found it, and at six weeks old, made a perfect retrieve. He was on fire.

I put him back in the pen and said, "Let's try all three again." Same as before. The first two showed no interest, but the scrawny little one—the one we didn't want—was all over it.

Even the breeder tried to talk us out of it. He admitted dog number three was the least desirable and had an aggressive, tough-to-handle personality. I was so conflicted that I called my friend Scott who's trained hundreds of dogs.

"You gotta take the one that chases the wing," he advised.

I paused. "But my wife's in love with the other one."

"Is your wife gonna hunt for you?" he teased. I knew that would never happen.

So we took the puppy number three home and named him Blue.

During the next six months, Blue destroyed our house and strained our marriage, but he is a champion hunter. He points instinctively, retrieves like a maniac, and possesses an off-the-charts drive. For eight months of the year, Blue is just a house dog that chases balls and leaves a puddle of drool while he waits for a peanut butter KONG. But take him out to a field or slough with pheasant scent, and it's on! Even at six weeks old, his nature was evident. An innate drive to hunt was in his blood, and the instant he's exposed to birds, he snaps into a different zone and *nothing* can pull him off scent.

## WHAT'S IN CONTROL?

While Blue has an innate drive to hunt wild birds, you and I have an innate drive to sin. We're naturally inclined to it because we all inherited a sinful human nature at birth. It's part of our makeup, and its pull on our lives is constant and strong.

Does that mean we're hopelessly bad, dismally enslaved to sin, helpless to do anything about it?

No. Not with God's Spirit.

The Bible says, "You are not *controlled* by your sinful nature. You are controlled by the Spirit if you have the Spirit of God living in you" (Rom. 8:9 NLT). It's a control issue—who or what is in control of your life?

Four months out of the year, my dog is in hunting mode and is released to follow his instincts without much control. But the other eight months? He's expected to rein in his impulses and abide by house rules. How do you get an animal whose instinct is to wildly hunt birds to be a nice, docile, compliant house dog for the better chunk of the year? It's not easy, but it's a matter of control. And it takes daily effort, just so we can coexist under the same roof.

Even as I write these words, Blue has wedged himself under my legs for a back scratch—which he loves—but then he also grabbed my hand as if it's a retrieving decoy. He doesn't bite, but it's a fine line.

The struggle to behave is just in his nature. It's also in ours.

## DISCUSSION QUESTIONS

1. What is the difference between a sin and a bad habit? Name a few examples of each.
2. When are you most aware of your own sin? Read Matthew 7:3–5. Why is it easier for us to see sin in others' lives than to see it in our own?
3. Our sinful nature exists despite the old life being gone. What signature sins do you struggle with consistently?

3

# THE OLD LIFE IS A DEAD-END LIFE

While on a twenty-mile bike ride the other day, I saw two other cyclists a quarter mile ahead of me. Of course, I wanted to catch up to pass them, because it was a competition. At least to me. I wanted to rocket past because I'm sixty-two and trying to prove I still have it.

I caught the first guy and breezed past him. But the second guy pedaled strong and steady, so I bore down and almost blew out a lung trying to catch him. After I finally passed him, I let up a little (because I was dying). But a minute later, he caught up with *me* and said, "Watch it on the right!" Obviously that irritated me. Plus, nobody passes on the right.

I immediately shot back, "You don't have to worry about me."

"And you don't have to worry about me," he said.

We were in our little spandex biking shorts, and I wanted to bump him into the ditch. I couldn't let him beat me, so I sped up and never saw him again. But a mile later, I thought, *What's wrong with me?* Sin is what's wrong with me, and it lurks just below the surface, filling me with disdain for a complete stranger who's just trying to enjoy a bike ride.

Whenever sin boils out of me, something dies a little.

- If we get angry and say hurtful things, our relationships die a little.
- If we give in to impulse spending, our financial stability dies a little.
- If we get drunk several times a month, all kinds of things die—including our judgment, work, health, friendships, and family.
- If we don't filter what we allow ourselves to watch or view, our ability to be productive or resist temptation dies.
- If we're self-centered and seek to accumulate things only for ourselves, our generosity dies.
- And if we cherish entertainment and fun as our ultimate goals, our purpose will die.

Anytime we give in to our sinful nature, something in our lives suffers and dies a little.

Paul wrote, "If you live according to the flesh, you will die" (Rom. 8:13). Not just physical death but the death of our relationships, careers, families, and futures.

## WHERE SIN AND DEATH BEGAN

God gave Adam and Eve freedom to eat an unlimited amount of fruit from an inexhaustible number of trees. Have at it, gorge yourselves, manage the garden, and enjoy all its succulent bounty. There was just one small prohibition: "Don't eat from the Tree of Knowledge of Good and Evil" (see Gen. 2:15–17). Why did God do that?

Obedience.

God created these human beings with a free will to obey or disobey, love or hate, trust or turn away. If they obeyed, they could enjoy all the bounty and freedom a life obedient to God brings. If they disobeyed, they would experience the darkness and death disobedience brings.

God always hopes we choose obedience and life, but Adam and Eve did what we often do. They ignored all the freedoms God gave—freedom to run naked through the garden, eat exotic fruits, fish the trout streams, and name the animals. Total freedom to do whatever they wanted—except eat fruit from one lone tree.

What did they do? They ignored all the bounty and freedom they had and focused on the one thing they didn't have.

Sound familiar?

## HOW MUCH IS ENOUGH?

How many of us have a perfectly nice home, an adequate yard, a decently running car—but it's not enough. We want *that* tree.

One night I was excused early from a church board meeting so they could discuss my salary. I left our office building to go home and noticed a new BMW, a new Lexus, a high-end Volvo, and a new Buick parked near my perfectly good VW.

My immediate thought was not *How nice for all of them*. Rather, it was *My board members all have nicer trees than me. Why don't I have one of those trees? Plus, they're in there discussing my salary. Are they aware I drive a used Volkswagen we bought years ago? Is my job less important than any of theirs? I wouldn't have to drive a dumpy ol' Volkswagen if I made as much as they do. They'd better give me a good raise, because I deserve a better tree.*

Really?

The truth is I am generously compensated and my car is perfectly fine—better than most. But in the few seconds it took me to walk from the office door to my car, I went from being perfectly content to being completely dissatisfied. I momentarily ignored all the bounty I have and focused on the one tree I don't have.

How foolish.

God has granted me a level of recognition through speaking, leading, and authorship—it's beyond anything I ever dreamed could happen. But in my darkest moments, I think, *Why don't I have his level of recognition? Or her number of books written and sold? I have a five-thousand-acre forest, but it's not enough. I want that lone tree as well.*

We see this in so many areas. God created this incredible thing called marriage and gave us the freedom to choose whom to marry. So we do. We search for someone, fall in love, get married, run naked through the garden, have kids, and build an amazing life together—everything we wanted.

But then we think, *Why don't I have that tree? I'm bored with what I have and a little unfulfilled. I deserve better. I deserve to be happier. Maybe I'm missing something more.* We ignore all the bounty God has poured into our lives, go for the forbidden tree, and invite untold pain, loss, and regret into our lives.

Adam and Eve thought what we often think: *I have all these amazing trees, but why don't I have that tree? What does God know? I think I know better.*

# WHAT DOES GOD KNOW?

The core of their problem was pride, and pride is always at the center of our sin—"I know better than God."

For example, God says to practice forgiveness (see Col. 3:13), but instead, we hold grudges and seek revenge. What does God know?

He tells us to be generous (see. 1 Tim. 6:18), but instead, we accumulate material things and spend only for ourselves.

He instructs us to stay sexually pure and not live together outside marriage (see Heb. 13:4), but what does God know about sex and marriage? We'd rather follow what seems pleasurable.

God created the world and everything in it; He had the first word, and He'll have the last. Yet in our pride we consider the Bible outdated and irrelevant to modern life, and ultimately, we pretend to know better.

The Bible says, "God opposes the proud" (James 4:6). In his book *Humility*, C. J. Mahaney wrote, "'Opposes' … is an active, present-tense verb, showing us that God's opposition to pride is an immediate and constant activity. The proud will not indefinitely escape discipline."[1] In our pride we seek worldly freedom because we think we know better than God. Mahaney suggested that what we get is active opposition from God that will ultimately lead to disaster and discipline.

The moment Adam and Eve arrogantly tried to elevate themselves above God, sin and death entered the world—and we've suffered from those destructive forces ever since. Try as we might, none of us escape the pain and loss associated with living in a sin-stained world—everyone gets sick, everyone has problems, and everyone eventually dies. But some people seem to incur an endless string of losses and wonder why they can never catch a break or get ahead.

Sometimes it's because of pride. We think we know better than God, so instead of submitting to His Spirit and biblical truth, we make our choices.

But the Bible says God opposes this kind of pride. He's not merely annoyed or simply tolerant of it. He actively opposes those who know what the Bible says about lying, cheating, drunkenness, greed, divorce, and sexual misconduct but defiantly do those things anyway.

If your relationships are bad, work is bad, health is bad, and the one thing you thought was good just went bad, is it because you think, *I know what God says, but what does He know? I'm gonna live life my way?*

If everything around you is falling apart or hanging by a thread, could it be that it's not just bad luck? Could it be that a habitual violation of God's principles is blocking you from the great life you could have? Your struggles may have absolutely nothing to do with your personal sin, but it's essential to pause and consider whether or not they do. Don't let pride cause unnecessary pain.

## FOUR DEADLY OUTCOMES OF PRIDE

Adam and Eve suffered four immediate outcomes of their choice of pride and sin. First, when they ate the fruit, their eyes were immediately opened, and they realized they were *naked* (see Gen. 3:7). Before, they'd always felt happy and safe. But for the first time ever, they felt vulnerable, exposed, and ashamed.

Next, they *hid* from God (see v. 8). Sin always causes us to hide. It separates us from Him and makes us feel as if we need to conceal something. Have you ever been there? You couldn't give your marriage, work, or friendships your fullest energy because you were too busy covering your tracks? Trying to hide something is like running a race with shackles around your ankles. The energy and stress it takes prevent you from running freely. If you want to be unhindered and excel, live in such a way that you have nothing to hide.

What came next was *fear*. When God found Adam and Eve, Adam explained, "I heard you in the garden, and I was afraid because I was naked; so I hid" (v. 10). Fear is always a byproduct of sin:

You shade the truth; now you're afraid of being found out.

You overspend; now you're afraid you can't pay your bills.

You lose your temper with a colleague; now you're afraid to go to work.

You let your emotions build for someone not your spouse; now you fear your marriage is in trouble.

You put success above your family; now you're afraid you've lost your son or daughter.

*Blaming* was the fourth outcome. When God asked Adam whether he had eaten the fruit, Adam blamed Eve: "The woman you put here with me—she gave me some fruit from the tree" (v. 12).

"Not my fault, God. It's that woman *You* put here with me. It's her fault, and it's *Your* fault, God. I was doing just fine until You made a woman from one of my ribs, and she's been a pain in my side ever since."

Adam immediately blamed others for his sin, and we've been blaming others ever since.

*It's not my fault. It's your fault.*

*Don't blame me; look at my parents. They're why I'm addicted, irresponsible, dependent, and unemployable.*

Or *It's my teacher's fault. It's because of my supervisor, my coach, Congress, the governor; it's the president's fault. I'm not responsible for my actions and life. It's that woman, that man, that idiot* You *gave to me, God.*

And I get it. Some of you have a much steeper hill to climb because your parents were legitimately nuts, absent, or abusive. Or maybe someone stole from you, cheated on you, or betrayed you in a way that left unhealed wounds. I get it, I've seen it, and it's not fair. Some of you have enormous obstacles to overcome that others have never had to contend with.

But blaming won't solve anything. As long as I blame someone else for my situation, I can't get better, and I'll remain stuck and helpless.

So if you're twenty-eight, still living at home, and under-employed because you quit school and struggle with addiction, I have a question for you: What are *you* going to do about it? This is your one and only life. Five years from now, if you stay on the same course you're on, where will you be? What step or action do you need to take to turn things around and reverse the trend? What book can you read; what person can you talk to; what class can you take; where can you volunteer and start to network?

Jason Day was number one in the golf world and consistently ranks among the top fifteen. For several months he even placed above Tiger, Phil, Jordan, Rory, Bubba, Dustin, and all the others. His net worth is over $20 million and growing. Plus, he and his wife, Ellie, have two sons and a daughter they adore.

But when asked about his childhood, Jason said, "My dad was a violent alcoholic." When he was ten and eleven years old and didn't golf well, his dad would beat him with closed fists.

How does someone overcome that to become the best in the world at something? Every son longs for connection with his dad, and every daughter desires a connection with her dad. When that's missing, the child feels a profound loss. According to John Eldredge, this level of rejection from the person you look up to for support and love creates a "father-wound" that almost never goes away, and it can derail a child from ever relating well or achieving anything.[2]

But Jason did relate and achieve well—very well. With the support of his mother and a beloved golf coach, Jason refused to let his father's abuse determine his life's outcome. He refused to make excuses or blame but used that pain as fuel to carve out a new life.[3]

And you can too. No matter what deficit, obstacle, or dysfunction you grew up with, you can overcome it and choose to live a new and better life. A challenging past? You can be done with that.

Adam and Eve's sin brought shame, hiding, fear, and blaming, and in their pride they thought they knew more than God—what does He know?

But God knew that sin leads to death, and the old life is a dead life.

## HOW WILL YOU CHOOSE?

As the pastor of a large church, I get a steady stream of emails that remind me of sin's deathly toll.

From a middle-aged woman: "I held a very strong, dark grudge against God. I lost my mom to lung cancer, I have an alcoholic father that I never see and an alcoholic older brother slowly killing himself, I struggle with depression, financial issues, and relationship issues. I feel like I'm sinking." (I wonder whether she'd feel less hopeless and angry if her father and brother chose to seek help and, whether they did or not, if she sought counseling for her own losses and depression.)

From a young woman: "My family and I have been estranged for quite a while now. A lot of pain and anger has set in my soul, and I thought revenge or taking my own life was the only way I could be free." (Family misconduct is cancerous to everyone, but bitterness poisons our own souls. What if her family members chose to repent? What if she were able to let go of revenge?)

From a middle-aged man: "My parents split. I got a girl pregnant. She left me and had kids with someone else. Eventually, I lost it all—my house, car, family, everything. It was darkness all around." (Starting with his parents, one sin led to another, an endless pattern of loss and darkness. What if he took ownership of his life, asked God to forgive him, and started making one good choice after another?)

This final email shows that even when sin brings death, we can always choose hope and life instead:

> Dear Pastor Bob: I'm a senior in HS. My parents divorced when I was young, so I grew up with a single mom and an alcoholic father. I'd see my dad only occasionally and wondered, *Do you love me?* My mom wasn't always emotionally available and often left me and my siblings alone while she went out. I laid awake many nights praying she'd come home safely, and I wondered, *Mom, will you be there for me?* I grew up without the curfew or structure that I wanted, and I wondered, *Where are the boundaries?*

Society tells us when you grow up with an absent father and a mom you need to take care of, you're supposed to feel unloved and vulnerable to excessive partying, drinking, and sex.

But I decided my relationship with Christ is enough. I can't pretend I have everything figured out, but I've decided I don't need to turn to partying or sex to [overcome] these suffocating feelings. I need to turn to Jesus. It seems so simple to say that, but I know someday I'll look Jesus in the face and tell Him I didn't need anyone else, anything else, but *Him*.

What a courageous girl! An easy and natural route would've been to fall into her parents' irresponsible patterns, furthering addiction and loss. But she's choosing instead to follow Christ and fight for her freedom. You and I can make that same choice, but it's a choice we must make every day—many times a day.

Even while riding a bike.

# DISCUSSION QUESTIONS

1. Adam and Eve had every freedom—except eating from the Tree of Knowledge of Good and Evil. What are some of the freedoms God has given you? Is there any "tree" in your life that you want but is off limits?

2. When your thoughts focus on that one "tree" you want, how can you set up boundaries and focus on what God has already blessed you with?

3.  Adam and Eve suffered four outcomes of their pride and sin: shame, hiding, fear, and blaming. Which of these four outcomes do you struggle with the most? What specific step(s) can you take to experience victory in this area?

4

# WHERE NEW LIFE BEGINS

I love golf. I love to play it, watch it, and study it. I love the stuff that comes with it—like the look and feel of my favorite ball, the Titleist Pro V1. You might think, *Isn't a ball a ball?* No. It's not. I won't even touch a Nike, Callaway, or Bridgestone. I also like certain tees—white, not brown; wooden, not plastic; skinny, not fat. Why does it matter whether it's white, brown, black, skinny, or fat? Because it does.

And I love the *thwack* sound when my driver hits the ball and the pure joy I feel in those rare times when the ball explodes off the tee 270 yards down a freshly mowed fairway. And we Minnesotans wait eight long, torturous months for that first swing.

Which is why I was borderline depressed last spring. After a 120-yard shot into the green with my pitching wedge, I swung, took a divot, and felt a sharp pain shoot up through my shoulder. It hurt like crazy. I told my golfing partner, "Something's not right … I think I'm in trouble."

I finished the round, but I knew something was strained or torn—and this launched a two-month search for answers. I couldn't bear the thought of being sidelined for a full season.

So the first thing I did was email my son-in-law, Nelly. He's a doctor, and because he's helped me before, I trust his advice. He researched rotator cuff injuries for me and then sent me five pages of stretching and strength-training exercises that I dutifully followed. But he said it would take weeks or even months to heal. I was in shock.

So I called him and said, "I don't have weeks."

He said, "Look. You can't rush it. There's a lot of stuff going on in the shoulder. Hopefully it's just tendinitis or bursitis. Give it two weeks, and let's hope your labrum isn't torn."

I thought, *What's a labrum?*

From there I became a fact-finding maniac. I researched "golf swing labrum tears" online and learned everything I could. I met with a personal trainer who gave me another five pages of exercises. I watched medical videos and read articles. I accosted personal trainers at my gym and pumped them for free advice.

When my staff caught wind of this, they asked how I was doing, but my reflex response was "Not good; *have you ever had shoulder problems?*" If they or someone they knew had, I peppered them with questions. Soon they quit asking me. I whined about it so much to my wife that she finally told me to "buck up, sissy pants." She always goes to the childbirth thing: "Try pushing out an eight-pound kid and then talk to me about pain." (I wouldn't willingly suffer that kind of pain in a million years.)

Finally, after a month without noticeable improvement, I went to a doctor. He examined my shoulder, ran some tests, and, after listening to my whining, said, "Bob, this is a First-World problem, not a Third-World problem."

My doctor is also my neighbor who rolls his eyes whenever I come in. Like a year ago, when he put eight stitches in my left index finger after I made a bad move with my hunting knife. When he saw me holding gauze around my finger, his first words were "Now what?"

Dr. Dale then sent me to a physical therapist who gave me another five pages of exercises.

By that time I had seen two doctors, four physical trainers, and one therapist. I'd read a dozen articles, watched four videos, and received fifteen pages of exercises. I was determined to overcome my problem and resume playing the game of golf as God intended.

But that would require leaving the old life, leaving my old exercise routine, my old way of warming up, and even my old way of swinging a golf club.

## THE GOOD THING ABOUT PAIN

Pain signaled that something was wrong. Pain was the sign that my old way of doing things wasn't working. And if I didn't change, pain would prevent me from living the good life.

Pain can be a valuable tool. It's the all-important message alerting us to pay attention so we don't further damage ourselves and others. Without pain, we could even cut, burn, or damage ourselves and not know it.

So where do you feel some pain?

It *could* be physical. But most often people suffer from a painful relationship, habit, memory, or past.

Whatever the cause, pain can be sharp, sending an immediate message to our brains that something's wrong. Other times it may be dull, and we simply try to ignore or manage it.

Some people try to medicate their pain with escapist habits like excessive working or exercising. Others use alcohol, drugs, pornography, overeating, or overspending. But if you ignore pain, it'll keep you off the golf course and, more importantly, prevent you from living the new life God intends for you to live.

So instead, let pain be a signal and say, "You know, that hurts. I'd better fix that, overcome that, heal that … be done with that." Thousands of people decide to stop what causes them pain every day, and you can too. By acknowledging the pain and deciding to do something about it, you can start living and achieving in ways you never could before.

Where does new life begin? It requires three steps: humility, honesty, and hard work.

## HUMILITY

Humility is the opposite of arrogance. Humility is having a modest view of oneself, and it includes a simple admission that something's not right and some weaknesses need to be addressed. It's essential to getting better—at golf, at marriage, or on a team at work.

Humility gets a bad rap, though, because many people view it as a weakness. But it's just the opposite. You'll never hear a person with weak character say things like "I was wrong. I blew it. I need help. Will you forgive me?" Only the strong admit their weaknesses.

Have you ever felt the freedom that comes from admitting you're not perfect? My wife can chastise me for forgetting or failing at something (which I do multiple times a day). But instead of getting defensive, I've started to jokingly say, "What do you expect?" or "Of course I failed—look at my upbringing." She thinks it's some crafty ploy to excuse myself for being irresponsible. But I'm not that smart. I'm just human. My teasing isn't an excuse, just a reminder to both of us to have grace even as we strive to do better.

Look at the statements below and ask yourself, *Are any of these true of me?*

*I feel anxious a lot.*

*I don't connect well with people.*

*I feel angry often.*

*I haven't been truly happy in weeks.*

*I feel spiritually dry and distant from God.*

*I keep making the same mistakes.*

*My life lacks meaning and purpose.*

If any of those statements apply to you, there's a reason. These trigger points of pain provide clues to a deeper issue. When something keeps hurting, robbing your joy, and preventing you from moving ahead, you have two choices. Either you can pretend nothing's wrong, continue living with the pain, and hope it goes away. Or you can humbly admit something's wrong and, with God's help, take the first step toward a new and better life.

Again, the Bible says, "God opposes the proud but gives grace to the humble" (James 4:6 NLT). It means God favors and helps those who admit they're not perfect and need help. He gives them grace—second, third, and fourth chances.

## *HONESTY*

Because of sin we all have something in our lives that causes us and others varying degrees of pain. But dealing with these habits and patterns requires honesty.

In his book *Integrity*, Henry Cloud said that facts are your friends. He quoted from Jim Collins's book *Good to Great*: "You absolutely cannot make a series of good decisions without first confronting the brutal facts." Then he quoted an acquaintance who said, "In the end, people get to where they are supposed to. If they make it, there was a reason. If they don't, there was one too." Cloud stated the hard truth: "Reality rules."[1]

If you're a parent, what are the facts concerning your kids? Are they responsible and faith filled or defiant, entitled, and rebellious? How about your finances? Are you saving and giving or falling further behind in debt? And your relationships—are they healthy and growing, or do you burn through one after another and assume everyone else is the problem? What are the facts regarding your diet, health, schedule, and faith? Are they healthy and growing—or sick and dying?

Just as there are reasons for success, there are reasons for failure. If you've been married twice and are headed toward a third marriage, there are reasons for that. If your relationships are strained and in conflict, there are reasons. The problem isn't out there somewhere; it's in here. *You're* the common denominator in every scenario. It's time to be done with doing the same things and expecting different results.

I never knew my golf swing was stressing my left shoulder, that certain tendons between the shoulder and rotator cuff are extremely vulnerable to inflammation and pain, or that lifting a one-pound weight strengthens the shoulder without building the biceps and triceps. These and other facts have become invaluable friends that'll keep me in the game.

If you don't know the truth about what's causing your pain, you'll remain stuck in the old life. So where do you start? With honesty and openness. Be reflective about your life. Think about what's not working or what you wish worked better. Ask yourself, *What's the one thing I wish I could stop, change, or improve?*

Next, find a soft chair, turn everything off, and sit for ten minutes in silence before the God who made you, loves you, and knows everything about you. God wants you to live freely and joyfully, so if you give Him a chance, He'll nudge you about what's causing pain in your relationships, family, work, or finances.

The biggest test of honesty (and strength) is to ask others to help you. If you have kids, they'll be happy to point out your flaws. When my son was ten, I said, "Dave, where do I need to improve?" He replied, "Are you serious? Let me tell you …" and then fired off five glaring flaws in rapid succession—mostly about my hurtful words and bursts of anger. You'd think I would've already realized those things were hurting my kids, but I was unaware. It took a ten-year-old.

If you're married, ask your spouse or a trusted friend what behaviors cause frustration and pain. That requires graduate-level strength and humility.

Or meet with a good counselor. It saddens me to watch so many people repeat the same mistakes that hurt themselves and others simply because they don't know what's causing the pain.

In our work environment we've tried to normalize honesty with one another. It's actually one of our staff values, and we call it *building a culture of feedback.*

For example, it's common for a staff member to prepare a talk, ask three or four colleagues to critique it, and then, after the talk, request feedback on how to improve. We've found that normalizing the practice of feedback takes some of the fear away. I say "some of the fear" because I'm always afraid to receive feedback on my talks, but that's how you get better.

We all have blind spots. We all have flaws in our personalities, behavior, or work habits that we can't see, and they block our performance and growth. But others *can* see them. If we permit them to give us honest feedback, they'll do us a huge favor so we can improve.

At a recent all-staff meeting, one senior staff member spoke about building this culture of feedback. Byron emphasized the importance of feedback, taught how to give and receive it, and then, at the end, modeled how to do it. It comes down to two questions: "What did I do well? And what could I do better?"

He stood in front of our entire staff and said, "So now I want you to tell me. What did I do well in my talk today, and what could I have done better?"

Nobody said a word, so he repeated the question.

Finally one brave soul raised his hand and commented on what he had done well. Byron said, "Thank you for that. Now what could I have done better?"

Silence.

The guy was surrounded by 250 colleagues who feared offending this senior staff person. Byron pressed harder: "Come on. Give me the gift of knowing how I can improve." What a great statement.

Finally the same guy said, "It was five minutes or so too long." And he was right—it *was* five minutes too long, and everybody in the room knew it except Byron. Now he knew.

Byron thanked him profusely and then said, "Someone else, what did I do well, and where can I improve?" He asked this four or five times, getting input from different people, until it became almost fun and normal. Can you imagine how a staff or business would improve if they learned how to give and receive honest feedback on their performance?

I'm actually quite bad at giving and receiving feedback. I don't like it; I get short of breath, and my whole body shakes. So I procrastinate and often wait until the pain is so bad and the damage so severe that it's too late to resolve.

But I'm trying. Whenever I sense pain in my body, spirit, or relationships, I try to pay attention to it. I'm trying to find the most competent people, ask for their advice, compare their thoughts, and—this is key—find the overlap. I look for repetition. When five competent people all say the same thing, then it's more likely you have the facts. You simply can't improve and find freedom from the old life until you go on a fact-finding mission about what's causing pain. So be humble, and be honest.

## HARD WORK

In John Maxwell's book *Intentional Living*, he wrote, "There is enormous magic in the tiny word *do*. When we tell ourselves, 'I'll do it,' we unleash tremendous power.... What is the number one catalyst for change? It's *action*.... If you take action, it will change your life."[2]

He stated he can't stand words like *desire, wish, fantasy, hopefully*, and *someday*. They're passive and defeating. Instead, he loves *action, purpose, strategy, definitely*, and *today*.[3] Active and winsome words.

Just as there is physical therapy for shoulder pain, there is spiritual therapy to develop our faith; both require a commitment to doing the work. You can get fifteen pages of exercises from three professionals, but just desiring and knowing how to get healthy won't actually make you healthy. You have to do the work. You have to follow the plan and do it right.

For ten years I religiously followed a three-days-a-week workout routine: thirty-five minutes on the elliptical, ten minutes of stretching, twenty minutes of weights, then two sets of twelve pull-ups at the end. I was the champion pull-up guy in high school and secretly measured my manhood by the ability to continue doing them. But three people told me, "That's the worst thing you can do for your shoulder. Stop doing pull-ups!" Furthermore, during therapy I discovered I exercised completely wrong by using too much weight, going too fast, and having bad posture.

Today I'm assigned these wimpy, embarrassing exercises with one-pound weights. I also do pelvic thrusts while lying on the floor to strengthen my lower back. They're borderline obscene and really shouldn't be done in public. But I'm all in and committed to staying strong. After humbling myself to accept the honest help I needed, I now know the work I need to do.

It took humility, facts, and action to abandon the old life of failure and pain and move squarely into the new life of golf and happiness.

# WHAT WILL YOU DO?

Why do so few people overcome their problems and become successful? We can access more information and expertise than ever before. But having information isn't enough. If you just listen, hope, wish, dream, or vision-cast, nothing will change and you'll be mired in the old life. You have to *do* something.

When I counsel someone through problems in his or her work environment, marriage, or family, I'll spend a couple of hours giving him or her the best wisdom I have based on a lifetime of experience. I'll spell out my recommendations as clearly as I can and plead with the person to take action. Often he or she will listen respectfully, nod in agreement, not take a single note, thank me for my time, and do absolutely nothing different. In my frustration I want to reach across the table and (lovingly) shake the person.

What are you going to *do*? It takes a "do" to get something done. Far too many people know better; they just don't do better.

I counsel many troubled marriages on the verge of collapse or already gone. It's heartbreaking. Nobody stands at the marriage altar and plans to get a divorce someday, but it happens to about half of all first-time marriages and nearly 70 percent of all second marriages.

The reasons for divorce are many. Some couples drift apart because of work schedules; some are torn apart by substance abuse, physical or emotional abuse, or infidelity. Some couples think marriage should be fun and fireworks 24-7, but then the reality of laundry, arguments, and annoying quirks hits. One or both thinks, *I didn't sign up for this; I deserve better; I deserve to be happy.* So they split.

But divorce injures people deeply. It wounds the spouses, who often describe the pain as being worse than death. The shrapnel of anger, loss, blaming, and weird family dynamics also hits extended family members. But children of divorce suffer immense loss. Psychologist Dr. Phil McGraw wrote, "If you're a single or blended family parent, your child's life has been shaken to the core."[4] Those are hard words to read if you've suffered through a divorce, and my intention is not to add to the pain. Sometimes divorce is unavoidable because of abuse, abandonment, or an affair. But people in our culture are increasingly shattered by divorce, and research indicates it's a contributor to all sorts of societal ills, including addiction, anger, violence, lower academic performance, and more.[5]

## DREAMERS OR DOERS?

That's why I'm direct with engaged couples. I officiate few weddings these days, but I agreed to perform a wedding for one of my friends' daughter. I'd never met the couple, but during the two-hour meeting to plan out the ceremony details, I grew anxious. I've had dozens of conversations like the following one, which illustrates dreaming versus doing:

I asked the couple to tell me their story and learned they both had been divorced and had young children. I probed further and discovered that a week after they met, they went on a trip together—three months later, she moved in, and they'd lived together for two years.

I then asked, "Have you received any professional help regarding your divorces to explore why they happened [facts] and the unique effects they had on each of you?"

"No."

"Have you read any books on marriage?"

"No."

"Have either of you had counseling of any kind?"

"No."

Sitting starry-eyed in front of me, they tried to reassure me, saying, "He's the most wonderful person I've ever met" and "She's just the opposite of my ex; she's so selfless and kind." I remained unmoved by how perfect they made their relationship sound.

I listened and smiled and tried to be pastoral. But then my love for honesty and facts took over, and I let it fly. I've repeated this so often to couples I could do it in my sleep.

I said, "I so badly want your marriage to go well. I want it for you, your kids, and your future. I don't want either of you to suffer the pain of another relational death."

They both nodded, and I continued, explaining, "Half of all first marriages end in divorce. But it's worse for second marriages; the divorce rate rises from 50 percent to 70 percent. That means you have a 30 percent chance of making it.

"And raising kids is really hard," I said, "but raising someone else's kids is the hardest thing you'll ever do."

They weren't smiling anymore, but since I had only one shot with them, it was now or never.

I was calm but measured. I said, "You're living together; perfectly acceptable in society today—but not to God. God cannot and will not honor or bless that. The Bible says that sex is to be thoroughly enjoyed between one man and one woman within the context of a committed marriage and that any other arrangement is outside of God's plan and therefore outside of his blessing."

I had their attention and, I hoped, their respect. "You've asked me to be a part of your wedding, and I want the very best for you and your children," I said. "So I'm going to ask you to *do* four things. I'm going to ask you to do them so you'll beat the odds, build a great life together, and be a blessing to each other, your children, and your families."

"First, I'm asking you to sleep in separate beds until the wedding. I *should* ask you to move out, and I usually do that with couples, but since it's been two years, I'll ask you in good faith to stay sexually pure before God between now and the wedding. As you demonstrate sexual faithfulness to God and each other, inform your kids why you're making that commitment."

I looked directly at him. "You have a young daughter. Do you want her sleeping around when she's fourteen or moving in with a boyfriend when she's nineteen?"

He shook his head.

I said, "Your daughter is watching every move you make and will follow everything you do."

I looked at her and said, "Your two young boys are searching for their identities. Their dad's an alcoholic and out of the picture. The only real man in their life is your fiancé, and the first thing you've modeled to them is that it's perfectly fine and expected to hook up and live together without the commitment of marriage. They've already been deeply wounded and face enormous odds. Who's going to lead them to church, expose them to Christian faith, and train them in the ways of honor, respect, honesty, and commitment?"

I softened my tone and said, "I want God's very best for you and your children, so please honor God and tell your kids why you're sleeping in separate rooms until the wedding.

"Second, you owe it to yourselves to call a good counselor. You should each see one separately to deal with your own stuff and then see one together to deal with each other's stuff—for at least a year. You both have troublesome patterns that, if not dealt with, will certainly put your marriage at more risk than it already is.

"Third, attend church as a family; never miss." I looked at him again and said, "Lead the way. Lead your family to church. Be the spiritual leader. You don't even have to know how to pray; just get your family up and bring them to church. Never miss. That will communicate to your kids that God and faith are top priorities. Plus, God will teach you things in church that you would totally miss if you're not there. Attending a great church will save you from a pile of heartache."

Then I looked over at her and said, "If he fails, then *you* lead the way to a good church.

"Fourth, read these two books." (Unfortunately, I find it all too common that neither has read a book on marriage.) I recommended my book *Get Wise* and John Gottman's book *The Seven Principles for Making Marriage Work.*

Then I prayed over them and asked God to protect, guide, and bless them. I prayed that theirs would be a marriage that others look at and say, "That's what I want. That's what it means to be in love and married."

I hugged them both, told them that I'd do everything I could to make it a fantastic wedding, and we parted ways.

I wish I could've heard their conversation on the way home.

I gave them four specific tasks because nothing ever changes by just dreaming and drifting. I urged them to stop living together, get counseling, attend church, and read some books. Four specific actions that could lead them out of their old life, save their family, and give them the best chance to beat 30 percent odds. They needed to be done with their own way of life and do something new. And that goes for all of us.

No matter who you are or how painful your life has been, you can do something to make it better. So be humble, be honest, and do the work—because that's how new life begins.

## DISCUSSION QUESTIONS

1. What is one thing in your life you wish you could stop, change, or improve?
2. Where are you feeling pain in your life these days? How have you tried to mask or medicate your pain? What do you think that pain is trying to tell you?
3. Which of the three actions listed below challenges you the most? Why?

   - being humble
   - being honest
   - doing the work

PART II

# AHA MOMENTS

5

## SIGNATURE SINS

I've said it before; I'll say it again—my dog is a sinner. I could fill page after page with his defiant and destructive antics, and although he's only five, he's already cost us thousands of dollars in ruined furniture and vet visits. He's a dirty, drooly mess who leaves a trail of filth and foul smells wherever he goes, and as my wife puts it, "There's nothing good about him." (She even threatens, "Never again.")

But I love him. We understand each other. Even as I write these words, his big blockhead lies on top of my feet as he rests by my side. Come this fall, his nose will lead me through endless waves of prairie grass and cattail sloughs in the Dakotas, and when that first pheasant explodes into the October sky and hooks the wind, all will be forgiven. It's as close to heaven as it gets.

But as I said, the dog's a sinner.

A few weeks ago my wife was visiting our daughter in Missouri, so I was in charge of Blue at home—which *usually* isn't a problem because of the electric fence lining our yard's perimeter. Not only will the shock collar jolt Blue's neck if he gets too close to the edge, but even if without his collar, he knows the boundaries and that he's forbidden to leave our yard.

At times, he's obedient and aware. When other dogs or people wander by, he runs right up to the line, wagging and whimpering furiously. Blue pines for every person, dog, car, squirrel, or butterfly that passes by his yard. But since he knows the rules and is kept in check with a shock collar, Blue exercises self-control, sits down like a statue, and yearns for that person or dog to come see him. Usually even the *thought* of getting zapped sufficiently holds him back—except for one thing.

The mail truck.

The mail truck is Blue's biggest weakness because the mail carrier tosses him treats as he or she drives by. The truck may be eight blocks away, but Blue has supersonic hearing. So he'll run up to the line as usual, sit, and wait. But when the truck comes into view, Blue starts shaking uncontrollably.

The other day he heard the truck coming, so I saw him run to the middle of the yard. He sat, waiting expectantly, beside himself with excitement. But this time his collar wasn't on, so I very sternly ordered, "Blue, you stay!" He didn't move a muscle. Still, when the truck was three houses down, I forcefully repeated my command. And even though Blue knew *exactly* what I meant, he didn't care. He sped off for the truck in a full sprint and left me in the dust, shocked and instantly steamed at his defiance.

I yelled like a maniac.

He didn't even flinch—just kept running full speed.

*And then he jumped into the mail truck.*

The carrier needed to deliver a package to our neighbor's door, but he couldn't even get out of his truck because my eighty-pound Lab climbed in his lap, nosing around for a treat.

My wife would've killed me, so I decided not to tell her (thought it best for her to hear about it buried in the middle of a book someday). The point is our dog's enthusiasm bubbles over for treats and the mail truck, and as contagious as his joy may be, alongside his endearing zest for life is sometimes an inability to control himself.

So now he's collared every minute of the day and sulks around as if he's being punished. He hates to be restrained, but this constraint keeps him from getting hit by a car, lost, or taken away by animal control. (Because—who knows?—it might even be illegal to jump headfirst into a government vehicle and slobber all over the mail.)

All in all, the collar keeps him alive.

## BIGGEST VULNERABILITY

Blue's best quality, his infectious joy, is also his biggest vulnerability. It amuses and infuriates us at the same time. I'd be embarrassed to tell you how often he's disappeared. Then after we yell for him up and down the streets like a couple of crazy people, some kind-hearted neighbor four blocks away will walk up to our house with Blue on a leash and say, "Is this your dog? He came down to play with our kids" or "He came to visit our party." Twice I had to retrieve him from *inside* someone's house, where he'd made himself at home. At this point our whole neighborhood knows our dog by name and knows the irresponsible owners who can't keep him under control.

I see it every day—alongside Blue's boundless joy resides a lack of self-control. It's his signature sin.

This is also true of us. Our strongest quality or ability is often where our biggest vulnerability lies. A home-run hitter in baseball will also strike out a lot. A comedian onstage may struggle to be authentic offstage. Women who are models on the runway can struggle with low self-esteem and eating disorders. Many of us who speak easily to large crowds are introverts who'd rather be left alone. How does this play out in your life? Alongside your greatest strength will often be a parallel weakness.

This section of the book is titled "Aha Moments" because the next four chapters guide us to discovery. They'll reveal patterns and help us recognize key moments and events in our lives that can move us out of the old life of sin and into the new life of greater fulfillment and joy.

Too many people drift through life as if in a fog and think little about their current circumstances. Resigned to believe they were born into a certain family at a specific time and place with only select opportunities—they think it's all fate. They figure they can't change their situation, so they accept it and meander through their lives without further reflection. Life dealt them a raw deal, so they give up on their dreams and try to make the best of it.

That's fatalistic.

The truth is we all were born into a specific family, time, and place that gave us certain advantages or disadvantages. Some of us got a great head start with parents who gave us access to every educational, spiritual, and economic benefit we needed to succeed. We didn't have to overcome broken homes, abandonment, addiction, abuse, foster care, homelessness, or generational poverty.

Others of us weren't so lucky. We started out with so many barriers it seems unfair, and those obstacles feel insurmountable. At the very least, breaking free from old patterns will require more time and effort. It'll demand courage, sacrifice, and a stubborn refusal to accept failure. It'll mean making tough choices about friends, money, and habits.

And more than anything, it'll necessitate tapping into a power that comes only from trusting Jesus Christ, who "is able to do immeasurably more [in our lives] than all we ask or imagine" (Eph. 3:20).

Regardless of background, no one is hopeless. No one is without options. Every day people choose to go back to school, ask for help, pursue employment, find a mentor, go to church, pray, and start reading the Bible. Every day people choose to stop drinking, stop using, stop cursing, and stop the cycle of violence, sexual promiscuity, and entitlement that was modeled to them. And every day people make choices that either keep them trapped or make them a little freer. With God's help and a willing spirit, anyone can start living a new and better life. Anyone!

## SIGNATURE SIN

So what is *your* signature sin? No matter how hard you try, no matter how many times you've said, "I'm never gonna do *that* again," you still keep on doing it? What's the destructive behavior that, when you look in the mirror after doing it, makes you shake your head and wonder, *What's wrong with me? Why do I keep doing that?* If your answer is "Nothing. Nothing comes to mind," then you're either not aware of it or not being honest.

Discovering it doesn't require much thought. When I ask "What's your signature sin?" note what first comes to mind. Because whatever thought or problem immediately popped into your head provides a great clue. That's probably your signature sin.

For me it's verbal misconduct. All my life I've struggled with saying offensive and hurtful things. And for those who say, "Come on. There's gotta be something bigger than that," let me remind you how lethal hurtful words are.

Proverbs says, "The tongue has the power of life and death" (18:21). Words actually can kill someone—and not just kill their spirit or self-esteem, although that's serious enough. But sadly an increasing number of people have become victims of cyberbullying, and after reading messages spewing out hate-filled venom, too many have taken their own lives.

James 3 compares the tongue to a tiny bit in a horse's mouth controlling the whole animal or a tiny rudder steering a whole ship or a tiny spark burning an entire forest (see vv. 3–6). James wrote, "[The tongue] is a restless evil, full of deadly poison" (v. 8). Think about your own life. I'll bet you remember certain negative words spoken to you—whether from a parent, sibling, spouse, teacher, or coach.

I'm not saying I don't struggle with other sins—because I do. I have satellite sins that seem to orbit my life and strike me unexpectedly. But the one with the most potential to ruin my relationships and derail my career involves my big fat mouth. I've said hurtful things to my wife and kids, and I've embarrassed myself in front of staff and board members with careless words. Countless times I've had to cycle back and apologize.

I've already mentioned a season when I mismanaged the pace of my life and was emotionally exhausted—which made me even more verbally dangerous. The tiny spark of my caustic, negative comments grew into flames that burned down relational forests left and right. The fire got so bad the church board moved in on it and said, "Either you change this pattern, or you're done."

In the seven-page evaluation document they gave me, which I reread every year, they wrote, "The [number] 1 focus in your leadership must be a growing consciousness to the weight of your words. Your words can cause more harm than you can possibly imagine."

This and their other carefully written warnings sparked an aha moment that has affected and begun positively transforming every part of my personal and professional life. While it's still my signature sin, I'm making real, life-changing progress.

What is it for you? What's the one thing in your life you just can't seem to stop?

The encouraging news is we're not alone in our struggles. The biblical writer Paul also had something he couldn't stop doing. In Romans he confessed, "I do not understand what I do. For what I want to do I do not do, but what I hate I do" (7:15). My translation? "There's something in my life that no matter how hard I try, I can't seem to stop."

Paul didn't end there: "If I do what I do not want to do … it is no longer I myself who do it, but it is *sin* living in me" (vv. 16–17).

He never specified what it was, but we do know it was some sort of sin he couldn't quite kick. It was his *signature* sin. I don't know about you, but it comforts me to know that one of the godliest men to ever walk this planet also struggled with a nagging sin. It reminds me that even the best of us struggle with something, so the goal can't be perfection—because that's impossible. The goal is to improve through a process of becoming aware, making corrections, asking forgiveness, and trying again.

# OCCUPATIONAL HAZARD

Some people spend their entire lives wondering why their marriage isn't working, why they get passed over for promotions, why they fail in school, why they can't get a date, or why they burn through one friendship after another. The reasons for such failure are varied, and sometimes other people are the sources of our problems—like when someone cheats on you, abandons you, lies to you, hurts you, or steals from you. These injuries are certainly legitimate and hard to overcome.

But blaming or faultfinding will never solve our present problems and ongoing failures. At some point we have to say, "What that person did was hurtful. But I will *not* let that person steal one more minute of my life." As hard as it may be, we must own whatever life we have and refuse to let what someone else did to us determine our future.

And that begins when we identify and attack our signature sin.

Where do you start looking? Start with what you're good at, because your signature sin often lurks alongside your greatest strength.

My greatest strength? Undoubtedly it's teaching. I've spent a lifetime studying the Bible and filling my mind with knowledge from great books just so I can turn around and share it with others. And I've seen God use my words to help thousands of people begin a relationship with Jesus and transform their lives. And that's my world. But all that knowledge has a dark side. My communication gift is also my biggest vulnerability.

I'm very quick with my words—dangerously quick. Arm that quickness with some biblical truth, and it can be lethal.

Have you ever been on the receiving end of this type of sin? Cut off midsentence? Corrected or advised by someone you know isn't actually listening to you? I'm ashamed at how often I've hurt people through a half-baked comment or a directive when I lacked full knowledge. So embarrassed, in fact, that I now force myself to follow five new rules:

1. Slow down. I purposely walk slower around the office. It prevents me from running around like an idiot blurting things out.
2. Lead with questions. I'm getting better at asking, "When's a good time to chat about ...?" or "Where are we with ...?" or "Before I give my opinion, what do you all think of ...?"
3. Soften my opening. How I approach things can make all the difference: "I could be wrong about this ..." or "Are you open to a little coaching?" or "Help me understand why ..." or "Let's take a walk and chat about ..."
4. No more swooping and pooping. My board rightfully accused me of this. I'd hear about a problem, swoop down like a seagull into someone's cubicle or office, spew verbal crap all over them, and then fly away. Never again! No matter how right or justified, it's never okay to swoop and poop.
5. Cycle back. I still make verbal blunders, but now when it happens, I get queasy in my stomach and bothered in my spirit. This uneasiness signals that I need to cycle back and muster up the courage to say, "I need to apologize for what I said ten minutes ago. It was a stupid thing to say, and I hope you can forgive me." I have yet to master this, but if you can do that, you're on your way to new life.

The other day my assistant perfectly modeled how to do this. She left a message on my cell to call her. Nothing urgent—she just needed to talk about a small matter. When I phoned her back, she said, "I want to apologize for what I said earlier. It was insensitive, and it's bothered me all morning."

Her words had been in jest and I wasn't the least bit offended. I enjoy a little office banter, and I told her so. But I also thanked her for caring enough about our relationship to return to something she thought was over the line. That's called *spiritual maturity*, and it leads to new life. If you've never done that, why not? What's preventing you from choking down your pride and asking someone to forgive you after you said or did something offensive? If you've never apologized (or seldom do), that might be a good place to start looking for your signature sin.

## GREATEST STRENGTH, CORRESPONDING VULNERABILITY

Take a moment to consider your strengths and whether you might struggle with a corresponding vulnerability or sin. Here are a few examples to jump-start your thinking:

- Strong leader? Can easily fall into pride.
- Life of the party? Never serious.
- Factual and measured? Often stoic and unfeeling.
- Empathetic? May favor feelings over facts.
- Truth-teller? Might struggle to forgive.
- Forgiving? Can overlook the truth.

- Favors the underdog? May chafe at strong leadership.
- Intelligent? Can be arrogant and impatient with others.
- Responsible? Often judgmental and intolerant.
- Tolerant? May lack discernment.
- Artistic? Often unfocused, impractical, unpredictable, and unstructured.
- Structured? May be inflexible or struggle to allow creative ideas to flow.

This list isn't exhaustive by any means, but it provides examples of how each strength has a corresponding weakness and sometimes more than one. And let's be clear—*we all have them.* It takes a level of discernment to discover our individual strengths and vulnerabilities, but if we can figure them out, we'll experience an aha moment that can push us out of the old and into the new.

Take a moment to evaluate yourself. Maybe you lose your temper at your kids' sporting events and rage at the refs. Maybe you lose control at parties and eat or drink too much. Or maybe you're married, but you fantasize about being with someone else. Perhaps you have an addiction to gambling or porn, and no matter how many times you've told yourself, "Never again," you can't stop. And maybe you feel hatred toward someone who hurt you, and although you've tried, you can't let it go.

What's driving all that? Do you know? Do you *care* to know?

Chip and Joanna Gaines, hosts of the HGTV hit *Fixer Upper*, shared in *The Magnolia Story* about their Magnolia brand that's mushroomed across the nation. But just eight years ago, they were a normal couple from Waco, Texas, trying to make ends meet. They lived in a small house, with little money and lots of debt—until a television crew showed up and followed them around for five days.

Yet many people don't know that Chip and Joanna are Christians and under enormous pressure that can be hard on their family. Several years ago, Joanna began seeing how her quest to make her house perfect was affecting her family. And she demonstrated the kind of self-awareness we all need. She wrote that she was working hard to keep their house looking nice, but it seemed almost every day she yelled at the kids for making messes, for spilling milk. She finally took a moment for herself one afternoon. She plopped down on their sofa, then looked down and saw that her beautiful snowy-white slipcover had little black fingerprints all over it. She wanted nothing more in that moment than to go yell at the kids for not washing their hands as she told them to. But then she heard the kids playing in another room, and all four of them burst into laughter. Their giggles were so full of joy that they pierced her heart. She said,

> I looked back down ... and I realized something surprising: *Someday I might actually miss those little fingerprints.*
>
> Right then and there, I knew I had been focused on the wrong things. And I realized I had a choice to make....
>
> So what if my house wasn't perfect?...
>
> I realized that my determination to make things perfect meant I was chasing an empty obsession all day long....

I felt as if a hundred pounds got lifted off my shoulders that afternoon. I remember sitting there on that sofa going, "Holy cow. I can breathe."

It all came down to a mind shift in which I asked myself, "What am I *going for* in life?" Was it to achieve somebody else's idea of what a perfect home should look like? Or was it to live fully in the perfection of the home and family I have?…

That day changed me.[1]

# AN INSIDE JOB

If a new life of joy and freedom has eluded you, if something keeps stealing your peace and sabotaging your relationships, there are reasons. You can actually choose to change that and to breathe again too. The biggest and most important choice is to begin a relationship with Jesus, who *alone* has the power to convict and change you. Sure, you can try to modify behaviors on your own, but I've found lasting change is an inside job that can come only from having a real relationship with Christ. Do you have that?

It's almost impossible to make good choices if your character is cloaked with sin. But when we believe in Jesus as the Son of God, as the Savior of the world, and come to a point of surrender, asking Him to forgive us, lead us, and change us, a new life starts to emerge. But it'll always require humility and a daily invitation to God's Spirit to keep working on us, convicting us of the sharp edges and giving us the spiritual desire and ability to overcome. By God's Word, the influence of other Christians, and prayer, we change our choices as Jesus changes our character.

In his book *The Road to Character*, David Brooks wrote, "Only God has the power to order your inner world, not you. Only God has the power to orient your desires and reshape your emotions, not you."[2] He also observed, "Your willpower is not strong enough to successfully police your desires. If you really did have that kind of power, then New Year's resolutions would work. Diets would work. The bookstores wouldn't be full of self-help books. You'd need just one and that would do the trick. You'd follow its advice, solve the problems of living.... The existence of more and more self-help books is proof that they rarely work."[3]

Willpower isn't enough to transport us out of the old life into the new. Our sinful tendencies have hidden sides that only God can see and that only He has the power to root out. Changing outward behavior alone falls short without inner transformation by God's Spirit.

But let me be clear—we aren't passive bystanders in the transformation process either. We must actively participate in the process of leaving the old life behind—and that involves taking charge of what we think and resolving that we're done with that.

## DISCUSSION QUESTIONS

1. What is one of your greatest strengths? How has God used it in your life? What is your corresponding vulnerability?
2. Every day people make choices that either keep them trapped or make them a little freer. Did your choices over this past week keep you trapped or give you a little more freedom? Explain.

3. Who has been affected or hurt by your signature sin?
4. When have you tried to change something in you through your own willpower? How did it turn out? Explain how asking God for help is the catalyst we need for change.

6

# ONE-TRACK MIND

What do you think about? What occupies your thoughts every day or even a good part of the day? Maybe for you it's been okay to daydream about another life or to get wrapped up in every what-if scenario. But I can say with 100 percent certainty that what you think about is who you are and what you'll become.

Ten years ago my wife's parents took us to see the Colosseum and walk among the ruins in Italy. A couple of miles away stood the magnificent Vatican City considered by many to be the most holy place on earth. We visited St. Peter's Basilica—an architectural wonder—and afterward the Roman prison cell where tradition says the apostle Paul wrote actual parts of the Bible. It was surreal to see the very chains that might have held Paul's ankles. And we gazed at Michelangelo's painting on the ceiling of the Sistine Chapel, and I can describe it only as breathtaking.

But what I never expected—and what changed my life forever— wasn't any of those things. What changed me for all eternity was a tangy, creamy Italian ice cream called gelato.

The first time I tasted gelato, eighteen new taste buds sprang to life. And from that moment on, the trip was all about gelato. Someone would say, "There's the Colosseum!" or "Do you see the Vatican?" and the only thing I could think was *Sure ... but where's the gelato?* Here amid the most iconic and historic sights on the planet, a creamy, dreamy wonderment filled my thoughts instead.

What occupies much of your thinking? Part of it depends on your stage of life. If you're a student, books and term papers consume your mind. If you're a young mom, your kids and their demands dominate your thoughts. If you work full time, your job occupies your attention at least forty hours a week, and that's just when you're on the clock. Many people think about their work, respond to calls, rehearse presentations, and check emails virtually 24-7.

I have hunting friends who think only about deer movement, fishing friends who think only about barometric pressure, and golfing friends who think only about tee times and putting grips. But they know as well as I that those things cause trouble when they become obsessions.

And while most of us have thoughts about money, food, and sex—none of which are bad given the proper context and proportion—when you check your personal net worth several times a day, schedule an entire day around food, or spend every waking hour fantasizing about sexual encounters, these good, ordinary, fine things no longer are good, ordinary, or fine.

Is anything in your life an obsession? Given what you watch on Netflix, hear on the radio, or spend your free time doing, is there anything you need to be done with?

Because something is amiss when you're gazing at Michelangelo's painting in the Sistine Chapel and all you can think about is gelato. I missed half of Italy because of a one-track mind.

You are what you think about all day long.

# THE BATTLEFIELD

When we enter into relationship with Jesus Christ, He begins to make us new people. So even though we still sin or fail, we have power through Christ to win the battle against sin. And the strategic place where this battle is fought is *in our minds*.

Scripture offers this insightful advice: "Do not conform to the pattern of this world, but be transformed by the renewing of your mind. Then you will be able to test and approve what God's will is" (Rom. 12:2).

We transform our lives by first transforming our minds. Another way to put it: "Take captive every thought to make it obedient to Christ" (2 Cor. 10:5). This verse presents a decisive *action*, telling us to do something about our thoughts. This means we can't passively watch a movie, indifferently read a book, or nonchalantly play a video game and expect to maintain control over our thoughts. You and I must cultivate discerning minds. Like warriors in a battle, we have to capture every thought—not just one or two thoughts but *every* thought—and bring each into alignment with the heart and mind of Jesus.

I don't do that very well, by the way. I capture some destructive thoughts, but I don't seize *every* one. Sometimes I'm very aware of my exposure to images and influences that could pull me into a bad place. When I am, I counter them quickly with prayer or replace any dangerous thought with a good thought. But many times I'm not aware. My mind can drift all over the place. Are you like me?

When our kids were five and three years old, we lived in Pennsylvania, and every night after the 6:00 news, the television sitcom

*Cheers* came on. So every evening we watched Sam Malone, Rebecca Howe, and Norm Peterson gather at a bar in Boston. But one night I specifically remember our kids coloring in front of the television when the theme song came on. Immediately they both stopped what they were doing and looked up. Then my oldest, Meg, began singing, "Sometimes you wanna go where everybody knows your name...."

My two kids were barely out of diapers, and they'd memorized the *Cheers* theme song. (The main message: the place to go to solve your problems is a bar. Not home, work, or church—but a bar.) We took them to church once a week, but *five* times a week Sam Malone and Cliff Clavin were educating them.

That's just one example of my television habits. I've probably seen every *Cheers* episode at least once and every *Seinfeld*, *Modern Family*, and *The Big Bang Theory* episode at least twice. What's weird is I used to hate *The Big Bang Theory*. In addition to its mockery of Christianity and overt sexual depravity, I thought it was stupid and juvenile—but then a colleague urged me to give it a chance. Now I sit there like a mindless rube laughing at Sheldon's fundamentalist Christian mother who makes all Christians look like idiots. (I blame my coworker.)

But seriously, here's the question: How much of our minds are affected by a steady stream of *How to Get Away with Murder* or *Game of Thrones*? When pastors like me say, "You should read your Bible," people internally reply, *But* The Bachelorette *is on.* What effect do you think these shows have on us? On how men think about women or women think about men? On how people view sex, marriage, or Christianity? Television has erased the line between right and wrong, and it's deadened our discernment. Marriage is now a joke, going to bed indiscriminately is the norm, kids are urged to question their gender identity, the notion of God and morality is laughed at, going to church isn't even a thought, and our families are in trouble.

Television is one powerful way to be conformed to this world, and it's so subtle we don't even recognize it. I'm ready to be done with that. If we're going to win the battle against sin, we can't accommodate these patterns any longer. The battle is fought in our minds, and truly God's Word—not TV, social media, or even our friends—is the only source for renewing our minds.

## WHY SHOULD YOU CARE?

I think the difference between those who fail in life and those who thrive is revealed in these verses: "Those who live according to the flesh have their *minds set* on what the flesh desires; but those who live in accordance with the Spirit have their *minds set* on what the Spirit desires. The mind governed by the flesh is *death*, but the mind governed by the Spirit is *life and peace*" (Rom. 8:5–6).

The thing is I don't know anyone who wants death. Nobody signs up for a dead marriage, dead career, dead soul, dead family, or dead future. People want life and peace, but Paul was saying the difference between those who rise and those who fall is their mind-set. Those who thrive have their minds set on what the Spirit desires, and those who fail give attention to what the sinful nature desires. One mind-set leads to life and peace, while the other leads to a kind of death in our relationships, families, and careers.

And Paul didn't mean "life" as in just being alive. The word he used for "life" is *zoë*, and it means "life to the full"—full of love, joy, peace, and relational and spiritual wholeness. Wouldn't it be amazing if you could have that? The fullest kind of life in your relationships, family, and workplace? So whether you're having a good or bad day, you're still content? The Bible says you *can* have all of that. The mind controlled by the Spirit *is* life and peace—life in all its fullness.

So if it's a matter of control, is sin or the Spirit reigning in your mind?

I'm a Christian and a pastor, and I read the Bible every day. Presently a stack of twenty-nine spiritually rich books towers in front of me—all of which I've read and underlined. Sure, I sprinkle in a couple of John Grisham or Vince Flynn books and, of course, some hunting magazines throughout the year. But if you look at my shelves that sag with the hundreds of Christian books I've read and reread, you may assume I fill my mind with things of the Spirit more than most.

However, at any given time, my mind can vacillate. In fact, I'm still shocked at how quickly anxiety, greed, or revenge can color my thoughts—and it can flip on a dime. Like when someone's driving faster than me, I immediately think the person's an idiot. But if the driver is slower than me, I think he or she is a moron. Or if I'm ready to board a plane, I get irritated by someone who noses ahead of me in line. Who cares about getting on the plane three seconds earlier? I do evidently. And if someone's slow to deplane, taking *forever* to gather his or her stuff, I wonder how someone can be so insensitive to others' needs. These reactions rise up instantly, and they bubble up from an inner world of thoughts and emotions either controlled by sin or controlled by the Spirit.

One mind-set leads to life and peace—the other to a kind of death in my spirit, my relationships, and my ability to enjoy the flight.

# WHAT GOES IN MUST COME OUT

"What goes in must come out" is more than just a saying. Author Tim LaHaye wrote that Dr. Gerhard Dirks, who at the time of LaHaye's writing held over fifty patents on the IBM computer, once told him, "I got most of my ideas for the computer by studying the human mind." LaHaye went on to quote this observation: "If scientists could build a computer that equaled the feats of the human mind, it would take a structure the size of the Empire State Building to house it."[1]

In *Mind Siege* Tim LaHaye and David Noebel noted this about the brain:

> Your brain is the most complex mechanism in the world and the most influential organ of your body....
>
> Your brain supervises everything you do, from the involuntary beat of your heart to the conscious decisions of your life. It controls hearing, sight, smell, speech, eating, resting, learning, prejudices, and everything else that makes you behave as you do....
>
> What we choose to see and hear and how we think (our philosophy of life) are the most significant influences on our lives, and they greatly affect all three major aspects of the mind: intellect, emotion, and will....
>
> Since *the eyes and ears are the two most important channels for communicating with the brain,* how you

employ these information gatherers largely determines how you think. And be sure of this: How you
think *will* determine the way you live![2]

LaHaye and Noebel essentially echoed what Paul wrote hundreds of years ago: whatever we put into our minds inevitably comes
out in corresponding beliefs, behaviors, and desires, and whatever
dominates our thoughts will—quite literally—determine the outcome of our lives. Other men throughout the ages have repeated this
same thought.

Ralph Waldo Emerson said, "A man is what he thinks about all
day long."[3]

Marcus Aurelius wrote, "A man's life is what his thoughts make
of it."[4]

Solomon recorded, "For as [a man] thinks in his heart, so is he"
(Prov. 23:7 NLV).

To be done with thoughts from the old life and to enter into a
newer life of joy and peace, we can take two actions.

## PURIFY THE STREAM

With the constant stream of information flowing into our minds
from television, music, books, billboards, social media, the inter-
net, church, school, and friends, we must realize every piece has a
value attached to it. Nothing is neutral; rather, everything tries to
influence us to buy, follow, believe, consume, or feel something.
This steady current will push us one way or another. It looks something like this:

Relationships  Smartphones  Movies
Podcasts  Billboards  Books
Websites  Bible
Music  Prayer
Facebook

## SIN & DEATH

Sexual Immorality
Impure Thoughts
Hostility
Quarreling
Jealousy
Lying
Outbursts of Anger
Drunkenness
Wild Parties
Strife

## LIFE & PEACE

Love
Joy
Peace
Kindness
Happiness
Self-Control
Generosity
Relational Wholeness
Financial Wellness
Contented Living

What goes in must come out in one of two ways. It will push us either toward life and peace (characterized by love, joy, peace, kindness, happiness, self-control, generosity, relational wholeness, financial wellness, and contented living) or toward sin and death (characterized by sexual immorality, impure thoughts, hostility, quarreling, jealousy, lying, outbursts of anger, drunkenness, wild parties, and strife). So we have to purify the stream. While we can't completely block every negative influence bombarding our minds, we need a continual flow of biblical truth and goodness flooding into our lives to counter the negative.

How do we do this? The Bible says, "Set your minds on things above" (Col. 3:2). To start, our minds should be on the things of heaven—on the things of God and His kingdom. And while we do that, we also must set them above in a whole other sense. Above what? Above the normal drift in society. Above the degrading and destructive values that television and most of our universities espouse today.

Practically speaking, to ensure the Spirit's control of my mind, I balance my love for Eric Church and Coldplay with a steady stream of Hillsong, Passion, and Eagle Brook Music. I balance my love for Vince Flynn and John Grisham novels with a constant flow of Christian books that teach me about marriage, raising kids, handling stress, finding my purpose, and growing spiritually.

People say, "But I don't like to read." That's no excuse—especially in this day and age. We can listen to audiobooks and podcasts on the same device we use to check our email and scroll through social media. Instead of listening to radio personalities or getting sucked into a half hour of Instagram stories, what if we clicked on the podcast app?

Whatever it takes, you have to find a way. Because if you hang around a bunch of Sam Malones, Norm Petersons, and Howard Wolowitzs all day long, you have to counter their warped wisdom with books and people that keep you spiritually sharp. Philippians 4:8 deserves to be taken seriously: "Whatever is true, whatever is noble, whatever is right, whatever is pure, whatever is lovely, whatever is admirable ... think about such things." Pastor and author Kyle Idleman wrote, "The best way to keep the bad things out is to fill 'er up with the good things."[5] It's impossible to just remove every bad thought—you have to replace them with better ones.

And most importantly, setting our minds above will require opening them to God's Word. As strained as some days feel, we must set aside time every day to open the Bible and plug into His Word. The psalmist David wrote, "Blessed is the one ... who meditates on [God's] law *day* and *night*. That person is like a tree planted by streams of water, which yields its fruit in season and whose leaf does not wither—whatever they do prospers" (Ps. 1:1–3).

The person David described has a constant stream of God's goodness flowing in and out of his or her life, and it's a blessed life. This individual is a tree loaded with good fruit, with a production and bounty that never ends. If the Spirit controls us, our lives will inevitably produce good fruit—His fruit—like love, joy, peace, kindness, and self-control (see Gal. 5:22–23). How does this happen? How can we experience God's goodness? Blessed is the person, fruitful is the person, happy is the person, successful is the person, who meditates on God's Word *day and night*.

The ways to do this are endless, but for example, what if each day you focused on one truth? You read it in the morning and think about it throughout the day. Truths like these:

- "I can do everything through Christ, who gives me strength" (Phil. 4:13 NLT).
- "Do not fear, for I am with you.... I will strengthen you and help you; I will uphold you with my righteous right hand" (Isa. 41:10).
- "When I am weak, then I am strong" (2 Cor. 12:10).
- Nothing can separate us from God's love (see Rom. 8:38–39).

When GPS technology first came out, pastor John Ortberg was driving with his wife in an unfamiliar area in a rented car. They entered their next destination into the device, and a lady's voice told them where to go—but John didn't think he could trust her. He said,

I was quite sure the lady in the guidance system was wrong. She said to go left, and I didn't go left. I went right because I knew she was wrong. Then, in a fascinating response, she said, "Recalculating route. When safe to do so, execute a U-turn." I knew she still was wrong … so I unplugged her. That is the beauty of that little box—you can unplug her.

And—would you believe it?—I got lost as a goose, which my wife enjoyed immensely. So we plugged that lady back in, and you know what she said?

*I told you so, you little idiot. You think I'm going to help you now?…*

No, of course she didn't say those things. She said, "Recalculating route. When safe to do so, execute a U-turn."

That is grace.[6]

The Bible is GPS sent by God, and it must be plugged into our brains to help us navigate this ride of life. We may think, *But it's so boring* or *I'm so busy with soccer, hockey, and basketball tournaments I don't have enough time for church once a week, let alone the Bible every day.* Yet we have time to tweet, shop online, and watch our favorite shows.

If we pack our lives with endless entertainment and activities apart from God, we'll have nothing streaming into our minds to counter the onslaught. And with no exposure to God's truth, no worship, and no inspiration from other believers, we'll find ourselves constantly blasted by the fire hose of Facebook and Instagram and by the banter of other spiritually starved people. Soon we'll wind up back in the old life of sin and bondage.

That is when our spirits sag, our marriages struggle, and our kids turn into selfish little monsters. Even darker, this is when we dangerously fantasize about escaping, fan the flame of an off-limits relationship, or question whether God is even real. All because nothing is purifying the stream.

If what goes in really must come out, we must capture every destructive thought and be done with relinquishing so much control to harmful influences.

## DEVELOP NEW DESIRES

Believe it or not, not everything we crave leads to life and peace. Some impulses—such as overspending, overdrinking, self-indulgence, avoiding exercise, or needing to win every argument—will never be beneficial or good.

So how do you develop new desires? "Take delight in the LORD, and he will give you the desires of your heart" (Ps. 37:4).

Notice this is an imperative, a call to action: "Take delight in the LORD." You have to *choose* to do this. If you decide to attend church, you're showing a desire to know God. If you choose to read your Bible or pray each morning, you're intentionally seeking God and delighting in knowing Him. If you keep pursuing such actions, your desires will inevitably begin changing as well. Craig Groeschel put it this way: "We pursue God with all our hearts until his desires become our desires."[7]

I understand how reading the Bible may not seem like the most exciting way to spend your free time. But if you stick with it,

I promise you'll start seeing things in God's Word you never saw before—things God meant *just for you*. And the more you read it, the more it'll become as essential as your morning cup of coffee or berry-topped bowl of yogurt. I can't emphasize this enough: you won't want to miss what God might say to you each day.

I'm reading 2 Kings these days, which can seem like an inspirational wasteland. But sometimes you have to slog through the rubble to discover the gold. I was sitting on our back deck on a Monday morning with the bluebirds chirping and my coffee already half-gone when I opened my Bible—not expecting much. I was feeling insecure about writing this chapter; my creative juices were zapped, and the blank pages intimidated me. Yet my eyes fell on 2 Kings 2, when the prophet Elijah knew his time was done and heaven was his next step. He had handed over prophetic duties to Elisha, and he said, "Tell me, what can I do for you before I'm taken from you?" And Elisha said something I'd never noticed: "Let me inherit a double portion of your spirit" (2 Kings 2:9).

There was the inspirational lift I believe God was saving for me on this exact day, at just the right moment, at the height of my insecurities. I lifted my eyes from the page and prayed, "God, give me a double portion of your Spirit."

I've prayed thousands of times for God to fill me with His Spirit, but this time, for the first time ever, I asked God to fill me with *a double portion*. This phrase, buried in the desert of 2 Kings, was there when I needed it. Just as God was faithful to Elisha, I believed God would give me an extra measure of His Spirit as I wrote, typed, and labored.

Now, as if that hadn't been enough, at the end of 2 Kings 2, Elisha, promoted to prophet status and empowered doubly with God's Spirit, got ridiculed by some teenagers. That is so typical, isn't it? You experience a breakthrough, you feel strong and inspired, and then *boom*. Out of nowhere you're knocked down by criticism, insulted by others, or sidelined by a flurry of self-doubt.

Elisha received plenty of criticism, according verse 23: "As he was walking along the road, some youths came out of the town and jeered at him." They made fun of him, yelling, "Get out of here, baldy!… Get out of here, baldy!" (Old Testament trash talk.)

You gotta love what happened next: "[Elisha] turned around, looked at them and called down a curse on them in the name of the LORD. Then two bears came out of the woods and mauled forty-two of the boys. And he went on to Mount Carmel and from there returned to Samaria" (vv. 24–25).

What? These kids ridiculed Elisha's hair loss, so he called down a curse *in the name of the Lord*, a couple of bears mauled them, and Elisha strolled away *as if nothing happened*.

I feel an affinity with this Elisha character. Anyone else? I'm bald, I'm getting up there in years, I feel insecure a lot, and I sometimes wonder whether some of my younger, hipster-type staff jeer at me and think, *The bald guy's past his prime*. But Elisha proves that it's dangerous to mess with bald little pastor types. If someone's filled with a double portion of God's Spirit, beware, young folk. He might have some bears you don't know about.

All of that came to me on a Monday morning, when I felt low and expected little from 2 Kings. But when God gave me exactly what I needed from the life of a fellow baldhead, my confidence revived, and my desire for God and His Word was enlivened all over again.

David wrote, "Take delight in the LORD, and He will give you the desires of your heart" (Ps. 37:4). God actually will give us the things we want and need above all else—like courage, hope, and joy. As we open our hearts to Him, we can trust He will move us toward these things, which our hearts have been craving all along. Furthermore, God will give us new desires that lead to life and peace. For instance, maybe you grew up hating church and hadn't stepped foot into one for years. But you began to prioritize church once again, and now you can't wait to be in a worship setting. Every human heart needs to worship, but you actually have to pursue it and delight in it for your heart to begin craving it. David Brooks put it this way: "One day you turn around and notice that everything inside has been realigned. The old loves no longer thrill. You love different things and are oriented in different directions. You have become a different sort of person…. You did it because … you reordered your loves, and as Augustine says again and again, you become what you love."[8]

When we delight ourselves in the Lord, He faithfully realigns our desires to be more in sync with His. Then one day we'll wake up and realize what we once craved no longer satisfies. Instead, we love what God loves.

## THE GELATO CHALLENGE

There's nothing wrong with breaking sales records and acquiring nice things. But there's also nothing better than seeing a college student put her faith in Christ and find new life. Nothing is wrong with season tickets to the Minnesota Wild or Timberwolves. But their worth in your life is not even *close* to that of the oneness you feel with your spouse when Jesus is at the center of your marriage. When you taste the fruit of the Spirit—love, joy, peace, patience, kindness, goodness, and relational wholeness—the sinful life loses its attraction. Just as ice cream does once you try gelato.

I taught our congregation this very message and went so far as to say, "Once you taste gelato, your desire for Kemps Ice Cream will die." Well, the national headquarters for Kemps Ice Cream is located down the road in St. Paul, Minnesota, and evidently the director of sales attends our church. He showed up at our office Monday morning and asked to have a word with me.

*Uh-oh.*

My assistant offered to run interference, but I said I needed to face the heat myself. When I walked downstairs, expecting this man to be mad, I found him standing in our lobby holding an *armful* of Kemps with a big smile on his face. Sixty-four pints to be exact! Flavors like sweet cream espresso mocha and strawberry rhubarb cobbler were part of the mix.

His name is Guy Fix, and he looks like a Guy Fix—kind of short, all smiles and winsome personality. He unloaded a dozen frozen pints into my arms and then ran out to his truck for fifty-two more. It was the first time we met, and all he said to me was "Just taste it." So I tried a few pints.

And it was shockingly good.

At the end of Romans 8, Paul tried to describe how good God's love is (see vv. 35–39). His love is so high, deep, and amazing that words can't even describe it. You just have to try it. David said the same thing in Psalm 34:8: "Taste and see that the LORD is good."

Maybe you've been pursuing everything except God recently. You've filled your life and mind with an endless whir of media, entertainment, games, novels, travel, and experiences. But has all that noise and stimulation led you to life and peace? Or to a kind of deadening in your soul?

The weekend after I met Guy, we opened a new campus in the Twin Cities and expected five thousand people to show up. I called Guy earlier that week and asked whether Kemps would donate ice cream to everyone who visited the new campus. He was all over it. So at the end of each of our four services, I looked into the camera that broadcast my message to the satellite campuses and said, "Maybe it's time for some of you to taste and see that God is good. Just taste and see. And for everyone at our new Anoka campus, you're not going to believe this, but Kemps wanted you to actually taste and see that Kemps is good. So they donated five thousand ice cream bars for you to grab on your way out."

The place went bonkers. The Kemps truck was out there with Guy and some recruits, and our staff and volunteers valiantly tried to keep up. By the end of the weekend, Guy was in tears—not because of the ice cream but because of what God had done. Six thousand new people came to "taste and see," and it was a sight to behold. Many took their first step away from sin and death and toward purifying the stream and developing new desires—and as a result found that God (and Kemps) is really, really good.

## DISCUSSION QUESTIONS

1. What thoughts occupy your mind consistently every day?
2. When have you seen your thought patterns affect your life, whether for better or for worse?
3. What steps can you take to ensure a steady stream of biblical truth and goodness flows into your life to counteract the negative streams?

# THE MIDDLE IS MISERABLE

Is it obvious yet how the idea for this book came out of my personal struggle with sin?

If I haven't made that clear yet, let me do so: I'm a devoted follower of Jesus Christ—but I still sin. So does each of my family members and friends. But if we identify our own signature sins and start controlling what flows into our minds, we can begin to flip the script. We'll gradually win more battles than we lose. Our relationships will improve, and we won't feel so beaten up and sad from fighting with people all the time. We'll be more at peace with God and with ourselves. And overall a newer, freer, happier life will emerge.

But for that to happen, we have to abandon the middle. Many people will say (or at least subconsciously think), "I *want* to experience a new life, and I *want* more of God. But I also want to be selfish, greedy, and dishonest sometimes." Essentially they want just enough "religion" to be good with God—but not so much that it affects what they do or where they go. Have you been there?

But the middle is miserable. Truly the middle is the worst place you can be.

## A LINGERING SMELL

A few years ago I was hunting in South Dakota. One of the dogs was on point, so I ran up to flush what I thought was a bird. But it wasn't. A black-and-white skunk stared back at me instead. Before I could react, it nailed me, and I reeked badly.

When I saw my dog closing in on this stinky critter, I raised my Benelli and didn't hesitate. (Some of you don't like that, and I get it. I have tremendous regard for all God's creatures, and I wish skunks and dogs would get along. But they don't coexist, and close encounters with coyotes and badgers can be fatal to a dog.) So in situations like that, you have to choose—because there is no middle. No amicable compromise.

Amazingly, after a few more hours of hunting, I kind of got used to smelling like skunk spray. At times I didn't even notice it.

Later that night, I was in my Super 8 hotel room. Without warning or even a knock, the owner's wife unlocked my door, barged into the room, and said, "You stink! You smell like a skunk, and you're stinking up my hotel. You gotta do something about those clothes." Then she turned and walked out. I could've been buck naked! But she didn't care.

So I dutifully took my clothes outside and piled them in the back of the truck to air out. Then I came back in and scrubbed myself clean in the shower. Problem solved.

But later that night, my hunting partner walked into my room and said, "Man, you *still* stink."

I said, "*Really?* I can't smell it." Honestly, I couldn't. I'd grown so used to it that even though others noticed the smell right away, I couldn't detect it.

That can happen with sinful habits and patterns in our lives. We get so used to something, we no longer notice it. Everyone else smells it—but we can't because we've grown numb to it. It's the same in our culture too. We've grown accustomed to some things we once said were wrong and destructive, and now we no longer notice how bad they smell. I'm done with that. I don't want to live that way. Who wants to be the only guy in the hotel who can't smell just how badly he stinks?

How does your life smell these days? Is something in the corner stinking up your life? Or are you so used to it that you can't even tell?

Most of us remain aware of the really big blunders, and we've mastered meandering around the edges of blatant sin. But what about the smaller stuff we think is no big deal? We don't blatantly lie; we just fudge the truth a little. We don't flagrantly use people; we just angle for favors. We don't commit adultery; we just secretly leer at attractive people. We're masters at living in the middle—between truth and dishonesty, generosity and selfishness, restraint and indulgence, new life and old life.

But we love the middle. The middle sounds so nice, so accommodating, and so politically correct. We applaud those who try to accommodate all views and lifestyles; diversity rules in thought and lifestyle. But sometimes there is no middle. Every time I hear a politician say, "We just need to come together," I nearly lose my religion. What does that statement even mean? That we should never disagree or voice an opposing opinion? How do you "come together" on something like abortion? Do we all accept the killing of unborn children? Same with gay marriage or allowing transgender males into female locker rooms. Is no debate allowed on these issues? Are dissenters simply bigots, haters, and homophobes—because they won't "come together"?

Someone's view of those things might differ greatly from mine, and I respect that. Everyone's entitled to his or her own opinion, but these are not simple "we just need to come together" topics. Each of these issues is based on deeply held beliefs, and often the middle is filled with moral and relational land mines.

As I write this, it's July 3, and the fireworks started in our neighborhood three days ago. Most of my life I enjoyed blowing stuff up with M-80s and cherry bombs. But now that I start heading to bed around 8:30, the booms drive me crazy. Just when I'm about to doze off, there's an explosion outside my window louder than a shotgun blast. It takes my breath away. And then it angers me. I want to scream out my window, "We live in a neighborhood, you know!" But I just lie there seething and scheming about how I might get even.

Evidently some people think fireworks and civility can coexist—that large explosions are compatible with quiet neighborhoods. But they aren't compatible. There is no middle. Even the law says so, and it's one way or the other. Either it's a quiet neighborhood where we respect one another, or *it's pure chaos, people!*

## THE MIDDLE IS POPULAR

The middle is where people say,

- I want a great marriage, but I also want to spend more time with my buddies.

- I want to fit into my jeans, but I also want a pint of ice cream each night.
- I want a healthy body, but I don't want to exercise.
- I want to invest money, but I also want that new car.
- I want to feel close to God, but I don't want to read my Bible or go to church.
- I want deeper friendships, but I also want to keep adding people to my ever-expanding social group.
- I want to have a happy marriage someday, but until then I want to sleep around.
- I want my kids to know that God and church are a priority, but they have soccer tournaments every weekend.

Psychologist and author Henry Cloud wrote, "Part of maturity is getting to the place where we can let go of one wish in order to have another. The immature mind 'wants it all.' But the truth is that the most valuable things [having a great marriage, a successful career, financial stability, and a solid faith] come with a cost."[1] Simply put, you can't have everything if you want to build a valuable something.

My friend's wife left him for another man. The divorced devastated him. For months he was in a daze, loneliness consumed him, and he didn't know what to do. So I spent extra time with him—listening to, consoling, and praying with him.

A year later, he met another woman, and after dating for a couple of months, they moved in together. He said he was lonely and deserved to be happy. Although I understand that, I also wonder— what if he trusted God with his loneliness? What if he believed God had a better plan for his life? What if God had picked out someone amazing for him and marriage was in his future? He'll never know because he decided ending his loneliness was more important than long-term happiness.

He's a Christian, and I used to see him often at our church. But ever since this happened, I've seen him less and less. I know he's drifting in his faith. This relationship is proving to be volatile, and it's affecting his choices. I haven't seen his kids or grandkids in church either. Here was a chance for a father to demonstrate relational integrity to his family, but instead, the message he sent was "It's okay to move in with someone who's not your spouse." His grandkids *might* make good relational choices when they grow up, but who knows? It's less likely now. I wonder whether he thought about that—or did he think he could choose this lifestyle *and* still be a good example to his kids and grandkids?

We've all been in the middle at some point, but the middle is miserable. The worst thing that happens in the middle—as my friend exemplified—is that our relationship with God wanes. Because when people are out of alignment with God, they want to avoid anything that reminds them of their disobedience.

## THE TENSION

Every winter my wife and I are privileged to vacation in a place where grapefruit trees grow abundantly. The downside? They're often in people's yards, and they're a huge temptation for me. Because I love grapefruit—and the fact that it could be free, even better. So when we go on walks, I'm constantly searching for low-hanging fruit that I can grab and take home on the plane. But it drives Laurie crazy, and you can feel the tension on our walks.

Now, in my defense, most people actually appreciate you taking their grapefruit because the fruit messes up their yards. So I'm actually doing them a favor—and usually I do get permission. But my wife's a rule keeper with very little patience for those of us who drift into the middle. So on our walks we have this ongoing argument over whether grapefruit that's hanging over someone's fence is private or public. What would you say? If it's hanging over the fence and onto the sidewalk, I figure it's public. But she contends it's private and gets steaming mad whenever I grab one. One day while she was chirping away at me, she brought God into it.

"What do you think *God* thinks of that?" she challenged.

I replied matter-of-factly, "I think God couldn't care less about that."

She shot back, "I can't believe it! You just *lied* about God!"

That made me laugh, which made her madder. (Have you figured out how our relationship works yet?) So she quipped, "You're goin' to hell!" And I lost it, laughing uncontrollably. To add an extra dose of hilarity, she even tried to beat on my biceps with her little fists—which sent me into the ditch roaring.

My dilemma is I want to live in the middle. I want free grapefruit, and I also want a happy marriage. But Laurie makes it clear—I can't have both. So I have to decide what's more valuable to me—free grapefruit or a happy marriage? It's one or the other. (Fortunately, I found someone who begs me to take his grapefruit. But it's still hard to resist snatching them on our walks.)

Here's the question: What's your grapefruit tree? What's that something you desire, but if you go after it, you'll lose something even more valuable?

Sometimes you can identify what it is by the tension surrounding it. If something doesn't feel right, if it makes you sheepish and guilty, and if *I shouldn't be doing this* crosses your mind, pay attention. Because that could be something God wants you to avoid so you don't forfeit something more valuable.

That said, until heaven Christians will always face a certain amount of tension between the old and the new lives. The reality is there's a constant tug-of-war between our sinful nature and God's Spirit. We get pulled between these two forces all day long, so it's not uncommon to land in the middle. We try to have a little bit of God but a little bit of sin and fun too.

It never works well.

Paul wrote that the acts of the sinful nature are obvious, and then he listed what they are: sexual immorality, impure thoughts, hatred, quarreling, jealousy, outbursts of anger, drunkenness, wild parties, and *strife* (see Gal. 5:19–21). That word *strife*, which some translations use, I'm not even sure what exact situations Paul was referring to, but my only response is *Ugh, darn, oh no. Strife* just *sounds* grating. It's the ugly kind of internal and external conflict that our sinful nature brings! These acts of our sinful nature lead to a deathlike reality in our lives that feels a lot like *strife*.

Too many people say, "Well, I don't want a strife-filled life. But I don't want a life void of fun either. So I'll take just enough of God to keep me out of the ditch." With that, they head for the middle.

But you simply can't go to movies like *Fifty Shades of Grey* and expect to stay out of the relational ditch. You just can't! There may not be an immediate effect, but over time the cumulative exposure to violence, deceit, profanity, and raw nudity will deaden your appreciation of anything real and weaken your ability to avoid pitfalls.

# A DIFFERENT PATH

If you're not a Christian and the list of sins in Galatians 5:19–21 is just how you roll, you probably don't feel much guilt over it at all. Because that's your lifestyle. Although it may be hurting your relationships, career, and future, it doesn't really bother you. You've gotten kind of used to it and numb to the old life.

On the other hand, if you *are* a Christ follower and say, "I want to be a Christian and be good with God. But I also want to be selfish, greedy, lustful, indulgent, and party with whomever I want," you just became the most miserable person on the planet. Because as much as we wish what happens in Vegas stays in Vegas, it doesn't. It follows us home. The gambling, partying, and cheating follow you all the way to the front door in the form of financial and relational loss, and the guilt can never be kicked.

When Laurie and I choose a route void of grapefruit trees, there's no tension because the temptation is removed. We walk along the path and simply enjoy each other because the trees don't torture me. I don't have to control my desire. In fact, I don't even think about grapefruit because I've distanced myself from it.

So if your weakness is overspending, overdrinking, or pornography, the closer you get to your source of temptation, the more frustrated you'll become. If you can still see it and smell it, the air will always be thick with tension. And while you're trying not to succumb to the temptation, peace will always evade you. That's because it takes so much effort and willpower to live in the middle, just one step away from grabbing the grapefruit. It's better to choose a different route altogether where you're not constantly frustrated by what you can't have and what you really don't want.

Which means it's one or the other. You have to choose between sin and death and life and peace. The Bible says, "Don't you know that … you are slaves of the one you obey—whether you are slaves to sin, which leads to death, or to obedience, which leads to righteousness?" (Rom. 6:16).

Paul used the slavery analogy because whichever path we choose—sin and death or obedience and life—will control our lives. But notice we have only two options: being a slave to sin and death and being a slave to obedience and life. We may *think* there's a happy middle, we may *wish* for a little bit of both, but it's one or the other. There's no middle ground here.

So let's pause and say you've decided to follow the path of life. That means you'll be a slave to obedience. You're bound and devoted to God. Doesn't that sound exciting? No. It sounds like a real drag. Paul wasn't commenting on the morality of physical slavery. He was simply acknowledging the reality that our souls are inherently bound to something, one way or another, and was encouraging us to choose God as our master.

Let me sum it up for you. If you choose the path of life and obedience, you can still hunt, fish, hike, travel, and play golf—only you do it without sinning. You can still work out, enjoy good food, and load up your carry-on with grapefruit. Because God's path isn't a boring path devoid of all fun, and following Him doesn't mean you change your personality either. I would argue it's a lot more enjoyable to go on a weeklong hunting trip with a couple of friends *and* be able to go home to your wife of forty years without shame. It's a lot more fun to go off to college *and* graduate without an alcohol addiction. It's a lot more fun to date in your teens and twenties *and* bring your sexual purity to the one you marry.

We're called to be free, but as slaves to obedience, we're also called to avoid indulging our sinful nature. What does that mean? We shouldn't use our freedom to go to certain places, be with certain people, or view certain websites. We're not free to be dishonest or cheat on our spouse. We simply are not free to do certain things—not only because God has explicitly warned us about their negative consequences but ultimately because of our devotion to Christ. And as we choose to follow and obey Him, I've found that God in turn blesses us and fills our lives with opportunities and adventures we never dreamed were possible. He'll do it for anyone who chooses obedience and life over sin and death.

## NEVER TOO LATE TO CHOOSE

If you're ready to be done having one foot in and one foot out—living a little bit with God and a little bit with sin—change is possible. Jacob found this to be true. He decided to be done with the middle and pursue obedience in every area of his life. He wrote in an email to me,

> My family has attended Eagle Brook for three years now, but I'm writing this email from a tent in Florida, on a military exercise getting ready for deployment to the Middle East. In my downtime, I watch videos of past sermons and enjoy your teaching as always.
>
> I've never been religious, Bob. Never. In fact, I attended your church more times in the first three months I started coming than in the rest of my

life combined. I believe I was born to a privileged family—it just didn't remain that way. I've never had a role model I genuinely looked up to. Certainly not my father. I had adult male figures, but mostly bad influences, especially during my teen years. Most men I looked up to were temporary, immoral, addicts, or alcoholics. It's safe to say my formative years were full of horrible choices.

But here's what I have learned: my bad choices in the past are not permanent. They do not define the man I am now or the man I want to be. Even though I didn't have the best role models growing up, I now know what *not* to do.

I've learned my daughters can have a father who breaks the cycle of alcohol and drug abuse that plagues our family's last name. I now realize I have to be the change that I want to see in my family. And no matter if bad things happened because of my past decisions, or someone else's, there is always going to be a Father who loves me and will always be permanent in my life from now on.[2]

Do you need to break the cycle of misconduct that plagues your family's name? Do you have children or grandchildren depending on you to get out of the middle—so in turn they can stay out of the middle? Because the middle isn't miserable just for you; it's miserable for everyone around you. Jacob led his family out of the old life and into the new, but he had to be done with the middle first. Are you done with that too?

# BE CAREFUL WHAT YOU CUDDLE

Pastor and author Chuck Swindoll related a story he was told about two women who were shopping in Tijuana, Mexico, when they noticed a distressed animal in the gutter. Bending down for a closer look, they saw what looked like a tiny Chihuahua breathing heavily, shivering, and hardly moving. So one of the women decided to nurse it back to health. She scooped it up and took the sick dog all the way back to Southern California.

When she got home, this woman tried everything possible. She fed it, cuddled it, and even slept with it—but when she woke to still find the critter very sick, she decided to take it to a veterinary clinic. As she handed the weak animal to the doctor, he stared at her with wide eyes and demanded, "Where did you *get* this animal?"

A bit startled by his outrage, she replied, "We were shopping in Tijuana and found this little Chihuahua in the gutter near our car. Our hearts went out to it when—"

He cut her off. "This is no Chihuahua, young lady. What you brought home with you is a rabid Mexican river rat!"[3]

What a mistake. Imagine her horror when she realized how easily she could've been bitten by a rabid rat? Whether this story actually happened or not, that's what a lot of us do with sin, isn't it? We get close to it, pet it, coddle it, and wonder whether we should pick it up and take it home. Solomon warned, "There is a way that appears to be right, but in the end it leads to death" (Prov. 14:12).

There's no middle when it comes to rabid rats, and there's no middle when it comes to sin. It might seem harmless and tame. If you're a Christian trying to live in the middle between obedience and life on the one hand and sin and death on the other, how's that working? Have you found peace? Are you free of guilt? Are your most cherished relationships intimate and safe? If not, I urge you to get out of the middle. Be done with that, because there's a better and freer life awaiting you.

## DISCUSSION QUESTIONS

1. Refer back to examples of the middle on pages 114–15. In what areas are you walking in the middle? What is preventing you from leaving the middle?
2. Valuable things tend to come with a cost. What are some of the costs associated with the following?

   • having a great marriage
   • having a solid faith
   • being physically fit
   • being financially stable
   • being successful at work

3. What fears do you have about leaving the middle? And what do you have to gain by leaving?

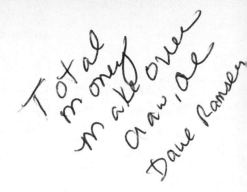

# 8

# TURNING POINTS

I've worn the same style of Levi's jeans that sell for $34.99 for forty years. But people started telling me I needed better jeans. I don't *want* better jeans. The beauty of blue jeans is their simplicity—they're blue, and they're jeans. But apparently it's not so straightforward these days. You have to choose from relaxed fit, skinny, straight cut, boot cut, flex, superflex, distressed, and stonewashed. Such a scam.

But one day I sat in a staff meeting next to a couple of musicians, and they both were wearing skinny jeans. And I had to admit … they looked good. When I asked them about it, they said with way too much enthusiasm, "Yes, you need to get a pair!" Excuse me, but I don't need to get a pair. They said, "Go to American Eagle and get some superflex skinny jeans!" There was no way I was going to American Eagle. But three weeks later, Laurie took me to some nearby outlets, and I tried on a dozen different jeans.

I went to J.Crew, Banana Republic, The Limited—no luck, and I hated it. My heart drifted back toward my beloved Levi's. I only had to grab a size 32/30 off the shelf and slap down $34.99, and I could be out the door.

But finally I walked into American Eagle. Of course, I was completely lost. So I asked for help. A polite twentysomething kid led me to a stack of jeans, pulled a pair off the pile, and said, "Try these." I glanced at the price tag and almost choked. But I took the superflex skinny jeans, went to a changing room … and something happened in that room that maybe has never happened before at an American Eagle.

I was born again. They felt amazing and fit perfectly. I shouted to my wife, "These are incredible." I came out and modeled them for her, and I think I saw a twinkle in her eye I haven't seen in a while. We were both sold. The problem was they were fifty-six dollars. American Eagle was offering a deal that if you bought one pair, the second was half off—but I didn't need two pairs. So I said to Laurie, "I'm gonna see if I can get a discount on *one* pair."

"They're not going to do that," she said plainly.

"How do you know?"

"Because that's not the deal!"

"Well, I can't pay fifty-six dollars for a pair of jeans!"

So she bolted for the car and left me standing in line with a pair of skinny jeans. I was very nice—I walked up to the gal and (with a tinge of pathetic whining) said, "I know if you buy one pair you get the second half off, but I only need one pair. So could I get a discount on one pair?"

She said decisively, "You have to buy two pairs to get the discount."

"But I only need one pair. Could I get a discount on one pair?"

She looked over at her manager and kind of yelled, "He wants a discount on one pair."

The manager called back for everyone to hear, "You have to buy two pairs for the discount."

"But I don't need two pairs."

"Well, then we can't help you."

"Then what if I don't buy *any* pair?"

"We don't care!" she shot back, and she was done with me. I wanted to hire her.

So I bought the jeans for fifty-six dollars. I couldn't leave the store without them, and I'm telling you—every time I slip them on, I feel like a different person. I never thought anything could look or feel better than my old Levi's.

But I was wrong.

Do you know anyone like me? I'm a traditionalist and minimalist. I scoff at fads and trends. Just wait long enough, and whatever goes out of style will surely come back around. I live by the adage "Use it up, wear it out, make it do, or do without." And I'm this way with my clothes, cars, shoes, appliances, and furniture. I take my lunch to work, drink the office coffee, and sew the holes in my socks—for real. So it's not natural for me to upgrade my wardrobe.

But trying on those jeans was a turning point that will change the way I dress forever. And like many turning points, I never saw it coming. I'm so stuck in my ways that I resist anything new or different.

But the Bible urges us "to put off [our] old self … and to put on the new self" (Eph. 4:22–24). You have to take off something in order to put on something new. I can't wear my old Levi's *and* my new skinny jeans at the same time. I have to take one off before I can put the other on. I have to take off going to bars if I'm going to put on being sober. I have to take off using hurtful language if I'm going to put on being kind. I have to take off being selfish if I'm going to put on being generous.

It can't be both. We have to be done with one in order to put on the other. It's a spiritual turning point.

## A SPIRITUAL TURNING POINT

So far the three aha moments to move you from the old life to the new are when you identify your signature sin, purify what flows into your mind, and avoid the middle.

But this spiritual turning point, the biggest aha, is like taking off old jeans you've worn your whole life and sliding on a new pair that feels so good you wished you would've discovered it years before. In fact, it feels so incredible—you can't imagine your life without it and hate to even *think* you could have missed it altogether.

This kind of spiritual turning point is often triggered by pain, loss, or uncertainty, and it leaves you desperate to hear from God. You don't know what He will do—or whether He'll do anything—but you're at the end of yourself and have nothing to lose. So you open up, you get alone, and you might even start flipping through Psalms hoping that some sort of word or sign will jump off the pages. But the main thing is that you decide to put yourself in a posture to hear from God. You open your heart to Him. You don't know whether anything will happen, but you're open.

And then God speaks to you—not audibly (I've never heard God's voice audibly)—but He nudges you by His Spirit. He prompts you or convicts you through a Bible verse, person, book, church service, or prayer time. And that prompting or "inner voice" is so powerful and real that it causes you to think about your life and relationships in an entirely new way.

You can also experience hundreds of smaller promptings in your lifetime, and actually these smaller nudges should happen almost daily as you read the Bible, meditate on a verse, pray, or talk with another Christian. An impression from God will come as an insight, encouragement, conviction, or simply a sense of God's presence and love. It may be subtle, but if you're paying attention, you'll know it's from Him.

In my experience I've found that four practices or disciplines open up the channels for God's Spirit to speak.

First, read God's Word. Whenever I read the Bible, I give God a chance to speak to me, and honestly, He does so with amazing regularity. But if I skip reading for a few days, it's equally amazing how I tend not to receive any insights from God.

Second, read inspiring books. I've had three *major* spiritual turning points in my life, and one of them happened during an overnight international flight. It was midnight. I was listening to the din of the engines at thirty-five thousand feet, and while others around me watched movies, played solitaire, or fiddled with sudoku, I was immersed in two books: *How the Mighty Fall* by Jim Collins and *Leading on Empty* by Wayne Cordeiro. As dramatic as it sounds, as I flew over the Arctic Ocean, God used those two books to save me from leading our church over the cliff of financial ruin.

Third, reduce the noise in your life. If you can't stand one minute of silence and are tethered to your phone, television, or computer at all times, you're going to miss God's promptings. I have to intentionally structure my day to include time without such distractions. When I carve out fifteen minutes, an hour, or even a day or two of solitude, I can tune in and hear God's messages more clearly.

Fourth, confess your sins. This may be the most uncomfortable practice, but unconfessed sin is a barrier to hearing from God. Isaiah wrote, "Your iniquities have separated you from your God; your sins have hidden his face from you, so that he will not hear" (59:2). If I've said or done something wrong or if I'm involved in a pattern of sin, I need to ask for forgiveness so my spirit realigns with God's.

To be clear, these major turning points don't happen every day. But a major spiritual turning point can happen in an instant, in an hour or two, or over several days. And when it occurs, it'll feel as though you've been saved or freed from something, as though you've had a breakthrough, and as though you're about to enter a new stage of life—a better, stronger, wiser, and more spiritually centered stage. Something was missing, but through this revelation from God, you begin to feel whole. Just like so many before us:

- Paul was blinded on the road to Damascus only once, and then he took the gospel to Asia and Europe (see Acts 9:3).
- Jonah was swallowed by a whale only once, and then he saved Nineveh (see Jon. 1:17).
- Jesus filled Peter's net with 153 fish only once, and then Peter began a new life fishing for people (see John 21:11).
- God spoke to Moses through a burning bush a single time, and then Moses' heart burned for God (see Ex. 3:4).

- David was anointed only once, "and from that day on the Spirit of the LORD came powerfully upon David" (1 Sam. 16:13).

You generally don't get blinded, swallowed, or anointed more than once or twice in a lifetime, but when it happens, it's a game changer. And here's the most amazing thing: God longs to do that for every person on the planet. He wants to move you to a level of living, loving, and relating that makes you feel grateful for every day you're alive.

# BREAKING POINT TO TURNING POINT

On the outside Sara appeared to be happy—a star student, open about her faith, with a pleasant demeanor. She even was runner-up to Miss Minnesota while in college. But inside she was Miss Miserable.

By age seventeen she was anorexic (starving herself) and bulimic (purging herself) and became dangerously thin. For the next four years, food was her enemy, body image was her obsession, and anxiety and depression were her constant companions. As she fought to keep it all hidden, Sara forced herself into a prison of loneliness and shame. Occasionally a concerned friend would ask whether she was okay. But she always brushed it off and said she was fine.

But she wasn't fine. "I felt completely dead inside," she admitted. Not to mention, the physical effects were alarming. Sara's weight was extremely low, her cycle had stopped, and she wasn't sleeping well because she constantly obsessed. "I lived in a state of *general unwellness*," she confessed.

The driving force behind Sara's eating disorder? Perfectionism. Maybe you know this, but when your standard is perfection, you're never good enough—never thin enough, pretty enough, smart enough, accomplished enough—and you're always asking, "How can I *be* better and *look* better?" Sara explained it this way: "There's never a stopping point because there are always more calories you can burn, more miles you can run, more weight you can lose. Then once you hit a certain number, you want a lower one. There's no stopping."

Doctors warned her, friends were concerned for her, and shame was destroying her. After four years the burdensome weight of her secret was crushing her. She didn't want to continue living that way, and darker thoughts of death creeped into her mind. Nobody knew. Nobody could know.

But when you keep something concealed like that, you allow it to stay alive and metastasize. Like an invisible cancer, it grows and eats away at your soul.

Yet we can trace hiding back to Adam and Eve. The first thing they did after they stole the fruit was hide from God—because they were ashamed. We keep things hidden for the same reason. We're ashamed of them, and we don't want anyone to know. But as long as they stay hidden, they hold power over us.

And then they start to crush us.

While she was home from college for the summer, Sara and her family planned a family fun day that included a bike ride and barbecue to follow. While this should've been an enjoyable day, Sara admitted, "I worried more about how many calories I was burning and dreading the family barbeque. I could do nothing to generate a sense of happiness." She continued her story:

That was the day I had a vivid encounter with God. I recall the exact time and place. I was reading a book called *The Search for Significance*, and I remember saying to myself, *My life has no significance.* In that moment all the loneliness and shame—the weight of four years of badness—came crashing down on me, and I couldn't breathe I was crying so hard. It was a breaking point, but it was also my turning point.

I opened my Bible and read a verse from Psalm 40 I'll never forget: "He lifted me out of the slimy pit, out of the mud and mire; he set my feet on a rock and gave me a firm place to stand" [v. 2]. That was me in the slimy pit, and I knew in that moment God was speaking directly to me.[1]

Sara emerged from her bedroom, and she didn't know what would happen next—but she knew she had to tell someone. So the next day she told a good friend and took the first step toward bringing light to what once was hidden. She then shared it with her family and saw a Christian counselor for three years. In her words, "When you bring something to light that's been hidden and people continue to love you anyway, it shatters the shame and it loses its power over you." But there was one more person she needed to tell.

Five months prior, she'd met a Christian guy at school, and while neither was looking for a relationship, a budding romance had surprised them both. When Sara went over to his house, she was visibly upset, and this young man assumed their relationship was over or she was seeing someone else. But through great emotion and tears, Sara confessed her struggle instead. She told him about her eating disorder and that if he wanted to break it off, she would understand. The young man put his arms around her, then assured her of his love and how he would support her for as long as it took to become healthy.

The reason I know so much about Sara's story is that the young man is my son and she's now my wonderful daughter-in-law.

Sara will tell you her struggle with body image isn't over. A single comment about "how good she looks" or "how toned she is" can send her back into those dark places of obsession. She has to make every effort to "take captive every thought to make it obedient to Christ" (2 Cor. 10:5) and lean on her husband and trusted friends for support.

I wondered whether the struggle with anorexia and bulimia is a spiritual problem. Sara affirmed that, saying, "Absolutely! I was reading through Isaiah, and this prophet chastised the Israelites for worshipping wooden idols and basically mocks them for trying to get this lifeless piece of wood to do what it can't do—satisfy and fulfill them [44:13–20]. It's just a hunk of wood; how stupid to think it can do anything for you."

She went on, "That's idolatry—when you look to something other than God to satisfy you. My obsession with how my body looked was my idol, but no matter how hard I chased it, it never satisfied me."

In the past Sara reasoned that one more workout, one more lost pound, or one more level would satisfy. What do you keep chasing? One more deal; one more sexual encounter; one more possession; one more promotion; one more trip, property, or experience? Once

*not yours to fix*

we get it, the newness and thrill wear off, the line moves, and the chase continues.

Because when you're chasing the wrong thing, it's never enough.

The day Sara gave up the chase and surrendered her emptiness to God, He began to fill her with His love and significance. It was a major spiritual turning point.

David wrote, "My soul, find rest in God" (Ps. 62:5).

Don't try to fill a void only God can fill.

Don't try to satisfy a desire only God can satisfy.

Don't try to meet a need only God can meet.

# EMPTY JAR, FILLED LIFE

The woman trudged to the well at noon, in the heat of the day. She never walked the dusty trail in the cool mornings with the other women—because she didn't belong in that club. She had five divorces under her belt, so it was better to go alone in the sweltering heat than face everyone's raised brows and disapproving glares. She had no real friends—just the men who passed through her life. And embarrassingly enough, she was on to number six—only this time he was just a live-in boyfriend. Tried a relationship six times, somehow failed six times, and her insecurities ran deep: "What's wrong with me? Why won't someone love me and satisfy my needs?"

So this was just another hot day and another lonely trek, but instead of finding herself alone at the well, she saw Jesus waiting there. Now, remember, this woman belonged to the hated mixed race called the Samaritans, and Jews did not talk to Samaritans. Plus, Jewish men didn't talk to women in public anyway—especially a woman like this. So when Jesus acknowledged her, even she was shocked: "You are a Jew and I am a Samaritan woman. How can you ask me for a drink?" (John 4:9).

Imagine this moment. Of all the women in that town, *she* got a one-on-one encounter with Jesus. She stood three feet away from God Himself—she saw God's face, heard His voice, and sensed His love. She'd never met another man like Jesus, *because there is no other man like Him.*

She questioned why Jesus asked her for a drink, and He looked tenderly into her eyes and saw through to her soul: "If you only knew … who you are speaking to, you would ask me, and I would give you living water…. Anyone who drinks this water will soon become thirsty again. But those who drink the water I give will never be thirsty again. It becomes a fresh, bubbling spring within them, giving them eternal life" (vv. 10, 13–14 NLT).

She thought He was talking about plain water, so she said, "Please, sir … give me this water! Then I'll never be thirsty again, and I won't have to come here to get water" (v. 15 NLT).

But Jesus wasn't talking to her about physical thirst. He spoke of spiritual and relational desires and said if she opened her life to Him, He could satisfy every thirst she had for forgiveness, wholeness, and healing.

All this time, she had chased men, trying to quench her thirst. Much like her, we tend to run after earthly things we think will ultimately satisfy us. But when we reach the end of our chase, weighed down by our loneliness, exhaustion, or shame, Jesus doesn't scold or shame us. Rather, He sits by the well and says, "I can satisfy your longing. I can quench your thirst. I can give you a new kind of love, joy, peace, and happiness that you can't get from any other person or possession."

This woman walked to the well that day to quench her thirst for water, but instead, she met Jesus, who quenched her thirst for wholeness. This was her spiritual turning point.

What do you do when God meets you at the well? When you sense God speaking very directly to you about your lifestyle? Jesus summarized the woman's history and pointed her toward the right path. She could've walked away and said, "Not interested. My life's not perfect, but I'm gonna live it my way and hope for the best."

But she didn't. The gospel writer John noted that she left her empty water jar at the well (see v. 28)—a symbol that she left her empty life at the well too.

We're given the same choice. When God meets us at the well and offers freedom from the old life of sin and shame, we can either turn toward Him or run away from Him. If you find yourself standing in the same empty place you've come to a thousand times before but this time God meets you there—what will you do? This could be your spiritual turning point, and it could change you forever.

If we keep reading her story, we see she raced back down the trail with freedom and joy and shouted to anyone who'd listen, "Come and see a man who told me everything I ever did! Could he possibly be the Messiah?" (v. 29 NLT). And because of *her* testimony, many townspeople ran out to meet Jesus and trusted in Him as their personal Lord and Savior.

God wants to bring every person through a spiritual turning point, not just to make us feel good, break an addiction, overcome a problem, or make us happy. That's just part of it. God desires to fill our lives with an ever-flowing abundance of His love—not just for ourselves but for the watching world. Because when other people hear about what God did for us, many will run down the same path to discover for themselves whether what happened to you could also happen to them.

During a recent baptism of a large group of people, one man stood out to me—midfifties, tattoos, physically strong, unshaven, a little rough around the edges. As soon as I met him, though, he got emotional. "Big day for you?" I asked.

He couldn't speak. I stood in the water next to him, my one hand on his back, my other clutching his massive forearm, as tears flowed freely down his face.

He finally choked out, "If I told you what this day means for me, I wouldn't be able to hold it together." So I simply asked him whether he's received Jesus as his Lord and Savior, and he nodded. He went down into the water, buried his sin in that lake, and came up a different man in Christ.

New life.

New love.

Living water.

Turning point.

Never the same again.

## DISCUSSION QUESTIONS

1. When have you consciously turned away from something you knew was wrong and chosen a new way instead? Describe what happened.

2. Which of the four practices mentioned—reading God's Word, reading inspiring books, reducing the noise in your life, and confessing sins—do you do well? Which one(s) do you need to work on?

3. Idolatry is when you look to something other than God to satisfy you. What are common idols for people today? In what ways might some of your struggles actually be rooted in a form of idolatry?

# PART III

# THE NEW LIFE IS
# LESS AND MORE

# 9

# LESS REBELLION, MORE OBEDIENCE

If I've learned anything in sixty-two years on earth, it's that life is a struggle. Some days are easier than others, and God grants us seasons of relative calm and joy. But from what I've seen, those seasons rarely last, and an unexpected setback or challenge often lurks just around the bend. That's because we all wage a daily battle against sin, and it can rise up in the form of relational tension, self-doubt, low-grade anxiety, brokenness, or heartache.

Even if you've been a Christian for most of your life—and even if you've avoided the hurt caused by adultery, divorce, alcoholism, abortion, or prison time—nobody skates through life unscathed by sin. Whether caused by our sin or someone else's, we've all experienced brokenness at some level.

Just five minutes ago my wife returned from her daily six-mile walk. She was on the phone with our thirty-two-year-old daughter, Meg. When my wife walked through the door, I overheard her consoling our daughter. "What's wrong, honey?" she began. Not a moment later, Laurie asked, "Why do you feel so down? What's causing it?" You could hear it through the phone line and pick it up miles away: brokenness.

Jesus said, "In this world you will have trouble" (John 16:33). In spades.

But Meg's not alone. Trouble and sin seem to trail me every day. Just when I think I've made great progress and gained a degree of victory over my anger, fear, greed, arrogance, or verbal spillage, I fall flat on my face and feel like a complete failure and hypocrite. One of the greatest challenges of being a pastor is trying to teach things I haven't mastered myself. Which is why I often have to say, "I'm in this with you."

So when I look at my life as a Christian and ponder Paul's words "The old [life] has gone, the new [life] is here" (2 Cor. 5:17), the reality has never been more clear. Sure, I'll experience promising seasons of self-control; God is changing me. But because I am a work in progress and God isn't done with me yet, I also experience the pull of sin and get sucked back into my old life. And when I do—let me tell you—feelings of fear and low self-worth aren't far behind.

So when Paul said, "The old [life] has gone," let's remember what's gone.

*Separation from God is gone.* Through faith in Jesus, we're no longer estranged from God, but we've become His beloved sons and daughters. That means we can go to Him anytime and ask for His comfort and help, as we would a loving father.

*Hopelessness is gone.* We're no longer hopelessly lost. Rather, we've been found by God, and He's given us access to His power, enabling us to defeat our sins and heal our inner wounds.

*The penalty for sin is gone.* Our past, present, and future sins have been paid for in full. We still fall into sin, but Jesus took the penalty and gave us the gift of full forgiveness.

*Bondage to sin is gone.* We still sin, but we don't have to be enslaved to it. Romans 6:14 says, "Sin shall no longer be your master, because you are not under the law, but under grace."

*And eternal death is gone.* Romans 6:23 says, "The wages of sin is death, but the gift of God is eternal life in Christ Jesus our Lord." We all face a physical death, but that will be a mere blink, a moment, a snap of the fingers when we leave this life and enter eternal life in heaven.

All of that's gone.

What isn't gone is the struggle.

The battle.

The grind.

The longing for wholeness.

What isn't gone are the lingering effects of brokenness and strife that sin (ours and others') has left on our lives.

## NOT A FINAL DESTINATION

I'm learning—and I hope you are too—that the new life is not a destination, a place you can get to and say, "I'm finally here." And it's not a state of perfection either, because that's unattainable for anyone on this side of heaven.

The new life is really less of one thing and more of another. Even in the face of our natural predisposition to sin, we can make progress—get better and live better. How? We have a new power and a new hope available to us.

You, however, are not in the realm of the flesh but are in the realm of the Spirit, if indeed the Spirit of God lives in you. And if anyone does not have the Spirit of Christ, they do not belong to Christ. But if Christ is in you, then even though your body is subject to death because of sin, the Spirit gives life because of righteousness. And if the Spirit of him who raised Jesus from the dead is living in you, he who raised Christ from the dead will also give life to your mortal bodies because of his Spirit who lives in you. (Rom. 8:9–11)

Paul didn't say "Jesus lives inside every believer" only one time—he affirmed that truth *four* times in *three* verses. This emphasis was not accidental. Paul repeatedly asserted that the Spirit of the risen Christ lives inside each believer, because Paul knew we'd have a hard time believing it. The same Jesus who made blind people see, sick people well, lame people walk, demon-possessed people free, and dead people come back to life—this same Jesus lives inside you and me. *And* the same power that brought Jesus back to life is available to bring back to life whatever is dead or weakening inside us.

## THE INTERNAL AND EXTERNAL BATTLE

God's Spirit dwells inside every believer, able to defeat anything else that tries to control us. That's why another Bible version translated Paul's words this way: "You are not ruled by your sinful selves" (v. 9 NCV). We no longer have to be ordered around by sin that deadens our spirits and ruins our relationships. Because—and only because—we have Jesus and His power to defeat it.

The problem is that our sinful human nature also resides within us, waging war against Christ's power and presence, so the temptation to sin remains strong and ever present. In addition to our sinful nature battling within us, we have an external spiritual enemy who's often underestimated. This adversary—Satan—is a living, thinking being who works day and night with only one aim: to destroy our lives.

What do his attacks look like? Sometimes Satan makes his move when we're exhausted, when our spiritual guard is down, or when we're about to take on a big challenge. If he knows we're about to take a bold step of faith, he'll often send a rogue wave of temptation our way to try to push us off course. The temptation is always tailor made for our specific vulnerabilities and could cause us to do something that would damage our marriages, families, careers, and everything we hold dear.

He truly doesn't play fair. The apostle Peter wrote, "Be alert and of sober mind. Your enemy the devil prowls around like a roaring lion looking for someone to devour" (1 Pet. 5:8). Our archenemy is unseen by the human eye, yet we can be sure he's relentless in his hunt and out for blood. He's searching for someone to destroy, and he'll wait for just the right moment to attack. So Peter scrawled a warning to us as Christians and instructed us to "resist him, standing firm in the faith" (v. 9).

Do you do that, by the way? Do you actively and daily resist the Devil? Because we have authority over him through Christ. We *can* defeat him—but it requires intentionally resisting him in prayer. That can look like this simple prayer: "Father, I come against Satan in the name of Jesus. Destroy him; defeat him; don't allow him to lay a hand on my life, my marriage, or my kids." And, Peter said, stand firm in faith. Refuse to let your circumstances sway your beliefs or weaken your hope. Faith defeats the Enemy. Paul confirmed that with faith "you can extinguish *all* the flaming arrows of the evil one" (Eph. 6:16). Not just some, but all.

This battle between the Spirit of Jesus and both our sinful nature and the Enemy will never be over here on earth. But while the battle rages, we *can* experience less defeat. Less of whatever has a destructive hold on your life.

Less arguing with your spouse over petty stuff.

Less anger over all the wrongs people seem to inflict on you.

Less obsession over your body shape or bank account.

Less anxiety over things you can't control.

Less self-loathing when you make a mistake.

Less yearning for that possession, trip, or deal you think will make you happy.

And while the new life is less of these things, it's more of others.

More filling of God's Spirit that produces a deeper kind of love, joy, and peace within you.

More trust that God will meet all your needs according to His riches.

More healing of your inner wounds through Jesus, who restored everyone He touched.

More intimacy with your spouse.

More patience with your kids.

More generosity with your friends.

More confidence in the person God made you to be.

More wisdom concerning your time, recreation, and relationships.

More peace that comes only from the indwelling Christ.

Ultimately, living the new life is really about living an ever-*newer* life. It's about progress—not perfection. Whenever the battle seems too hard or our struggles appear insurmountable, we fight back with truth and remember 2 Peter 1:3–4: we have everything we need (the person and power of Jesus inside us) to participate in the divine nature (new life) and escape the world's corruption (old life), which is caused by evil desires (our sinful nature).

Is there any better news than this? We have everything we need to live in the flow of the new life and avoid the entanglements of the old. It's there, it's available, and we have the power to be done with anything that holds us back.

But practically speaking … how?

## FOUR TENSIONS, ONE PATH

In my life I've noticed four main tensions or battlegrounds where the war between the old and the new lives is fought. Four main tensions I must constantly monitor. And they determine whether I'm losing or gaining ground. They are the tensions between rebellion and obedience (the topic of this chapter), possessions and people, selfishness and sacrifice, and obsession and devotion. When I experience less of the negatives and more of the positives, I'm at peace with myself, God, and others. But when the pendulum swings the other way, I face the opposite effect—I'm not at peace with myself, God, and others. In this truth we discover the pathway to escape the struggle of the old life. So how do we start down this path? It begins with a little gardening.

## *PULLING WEEDS*

I see *Jesus Calling* by Sarah Young sitting on end tables, kitchen counters, and mantels more often than any other book. Sarah suffers from a physical illness that would crush the spirits of many, but it has deepened her passion for Jesus, and her writings now drip with devotion. This morning I read these words: "I [Jesus] have promised *to meet all your needs according to My glorious riches.* Your deepest, most constant need is for My Peace. I have planted Peace in the garden of your heart, where I live, but there are weeds growing there too: pride, worry, selfishness, unbelief."[1]

Don't we all want peace? I know I do. If we could have peace of mind and heart, we could face the world. We could smile and breathe and laugh again.

But there are weeds.

## *SEEDS OF REBELLION*

A few months ago when my wife and I were on vacation, I drove to a nearby golf course. Most courses don't charge fees to use their practice greens, so I putted for a while—but then I couldn't stand it. I kept peering over at the driving range, and I knew I had to hit some balls. Now, you're supposed to pay for *that*, but I surmised, *You know, it's late in the day. No one's around. I'll just drift over and hit a few balls—no problem.*

So I walked over, quickly grabbed my pitching wedge, and put a good swing on it. It felt so good I had to hit another. Then another. Somehow I worked my way through my entire bag until I got to my driver. Now, let me tell you—there's nothing like smashing a golf ball with your driver after four months of winter, and this moment did not disappoint. It was breathtaking.

But the whole time I couldn't suppress guilt inside. I thought, *How can something that feels so good be so bad?*

Have you ever asked yourself that question? Usually it's a sign that something's amiss—along with three other predictors.

First, I rationalized. I reasoned, *It's late. I'm not bothering anyone— no problem*, and I tried to convince myself that something was okay. When it wasn't.

Second, I minimized. I thought, *This is minor. People do far worse! Why am I making it a big deal?* But whenever I try to minimize my rebellion or compare my sin with that of thieves, murderers, or people who shoot fireworks in quiet neighborhoods, I know I'm in trouble.

Third, I tried to outrun my conscience by swinging harder and faster. After all, if I just stay busy and fill up every inch of my life with activity, then I don't have to think about whatever sin I got entangled in.

I can always tell I'm flirting with the old life when I find myself rationalizing, minimizing, and trying to outrun my conscience.

So my action gnawed at me. I was out of the Minnesota cold, standing on lush green grass, feeling the warm desert breeze on my face, and watching the flight of my golf ball against the backdrop of palm trees and sunlit mountains. It was perfect.

But I wasn't perfect. I love golf more than almost anything, but I wasn't loving it that evening.

And then the next day I got deathly sick with the flu. Generally I don't believe God punishes people like that. But maybe this time He wanted to get my attention. I actually sensed God saying, "Really, Merritt? In order to save twenty bucks, you broke the rules? Here are five days of sick so you can think about it." And that's exactly what happened. I was so sick—I couldn't read, watch television, or get out of bed for the better part of the week. All I could do was think about my choice.

In fact, my sin bothered me so much that I drove back to the course, walked up to the desk, and said to the attendant, "I was over here the other night on your driving range, but I didn't pay. So I wanna pay."

He just blinked back at me. "What?"

I pointed to the driving range. "I was over here, and I hit some balls. I didn't pay."

He said, "Oh man, don't worry about it!"

I wasn't backing down. "No, I really need to pay."

He shook his head, then said, "The fact that you came back and offered to pay is so *honorable*. This one's on us."

Right. I was honorable. But first I was dishonorable. I was rebellious. I was actually stealing, and I knew it, but I went ahead and did it anyway. And the whole time I was doing it, I felt miserable and could actually feel the internal conflict between rebellion and obedience. I had twitches of fear and hoped no one from the pro shop would wander over, engage me in conversation, and ask what I did for a living.

The good news, though, is I finally made it right. I finally confessed and shifted from rebellion to obedience.

The other good news is that sort of thing happens less and less frequently. I've grown. I'm quicker to detect the danger spots. I'm more aware of what Peter called "evil desires" that tempt me to cross lines (2 Pet. 1:4), and I'm more resolved to fight back against those things threatening to keep me stuck in the old life of guilt and shame.

## AN UNLIKELY PLACE TO LOOK FOR WEEDS

Here's the shocker: your greatest vulnerability to rebellion will usually be connected in some way to your greatest desires.

Now, don't be mistaken—desire in and of itself isn't bad. We all have legitimate needs that come with corresponding desires that help get those needs met. We nee nutrients, and God created a corresponding desire for food. We experience loneliness, and God created a corresponding desire for friendship. We experience sexual urges, and God created a corresponding desire for intimacy and lovemaking. We experience stress, and God created a corresponding desire for recreation.

I'll use recreation to explain how something good becomes a vulnerability. Recreation is how we restore—or re-create—our bodies and souls. So we read, walk, bird, cook, or golf, and these are all good and healthy activities (desires) God invites us to enjoy.

But one of my greatest vulnerabilities to rebellion connects to this desire for recreation, specifically my love for golf. It can occupy my mind, drive my decisions, and dictate my moods. If I play well, I'm happy; if I play poorly, I'm grumpy. In addition, golf is time consuming and expensive. At times I've neglected my wife and family to get on the course. And because it's so expensive, I'm tempted to cut financial corners. These are trouble spots that make me vulnerable to rebellion—a vulnerability that started early.

## CHILDHOOD WEEDS

My dad, a pastor too, received numerous invitations to golf, and often his green fees were taken care of. At one point he was even gifted a free membership to a local course.

But then something shifted. These freebies morphed into expectations, so free golf was assumed. And if it was free for the pastor, why not for his two boys as well? I remember being dropped off at the golf course, walking up to the tee box, and just letting it fly. Without permission I played a full round of golf on the house without the house ever knowing. So the weed of taking things that weren't mine was planted early—especially with golf.

Do you remember who else struggled with taking something that wasn't theirs? Begun long before my dad, this battle started early—very early. In fact, this was the first sin ever committed. Adam and Eve took some fruit that wasn't theirs, and this single rebellious act led to banishment from the garden, shame over their nakedness, pain in childbirth, a lifetime of hard labor, and cold-blooded murder in their own family. Remember how God told them—explicitly—not to take the fruit (see Gen. 2:17)? They chose rebellion over obedience and lost everything that brought them peace and joy.

God offers us the peace that comes with obedience, but weeds grow in the garden of our hearts; they weigh on our spirits, making us heartsick. So we have to pull the weed of rebellion, confront our dishonesty, and march back to the golf course. After five days of misery, I knew I had to pull the weed and be done with that. Maybe it's clear to you now too—the only pathway to freedom is to become obedient.

# THERE'S A DO TO BEING DONE

Once I chose obedience, I actually had to get in the car, drive to the golf course, walk into the pro shop, pull out my wallet, and confess. Because obedience requires actions. It's not just having nice thoughts, having good intentions, or hoping something changes; obedience always involves *doing* things.

Paul wrote, "Work hard to show the results of your salvation, *obeying* God with deep reverence and fear. For God is working in you, giving you the desire and the power to *do* what pleases him" (Phil. 2:12–13 NLT). Notice how it's both God's work *and* our work. "God is working in you" so that you have "the desire and the power to do what pleases him." There is a do to being done with it.

When I chose to obey God at the golf course that day, I experienced immediate relief and release. Something broke free inside my spirit. A cloud of guilt lifted, and I felt God's smile again. I also sensed the spirit of rebellion weaken in me. When we find the courage to confront sin and take steps to act obediently, we can feel our self-control strengthen. The tension between rebellion and obedience remains, and weeds tend to grow back again. But I'm quicker at recognizing when I'm in the weeds and what I need to do to get out of them.

Sometimes it's hard to tell when we slip back into the weeds of rebellion, but we can always check our level of peace if we're unsure. Is my soul at rest, or is my soul troubled by anxiety and fear? Am I experiencing peace of mind, or has God's peace leaked out of my life? Every time my wife asks me to change the channel from the riveting golf match to something she prefers on HGTV, I wrestle with a spirit of rebellion. And sometimes rebellion wins. Other times obedience wins.

Rebellion is whenever you *know* something is wrong—when you know you should go one way—but a spirit of defiance surges to the surface and you take off the opposite way. You're headed for the weeds of anxiety, fear, and loss. Like in the following examples:

- You know you should go straight home from work, but you join your buddies at the bar instead. Refuse that, and your rebellion will weaken.
- You know you should offer an apology, but you remain quiet, minimize the offense, and let the relationship turn cold. Practice saying "I'm sorry," and obedience will strengthen.
- You know you should avoid a certain coworker, but you find excuses to walk past her desk numerous times a day even though you're married. Avoid that corridor, and your rebellion will wane.
- You know you shouldn't pad your expense account, but it becomes a weedy habit. Vow to no longer take anything that isn't yours, and this impulse will weaken while a freeing pattern of honesty will strengthen.

Lurking behind our greatest desires are pockets of temptation and surges of rebellion choking out the new life. Be done with their stranglehold on your life, and pull those weeds out—for good.

# FREE AS A BIRD

On this same trip, my wife and I left the patio door open while we sat outside and read. The moment was peaceful until a hummingbird flew into the house, and panic instantly arose. He bounced around until he trapped himself between a large window and its blinds. I said to Laurie, "Maybe he'll find his own way out." We watched him for a minute, his wings beating and his body banging against the window, and we felt helpless. He could see where he wanted to go, but he couldn't escape. He just kept beating and banging in a desperate effort to be free.

Do you ever feel that way? You see the life you want, but you can't seem to reach it? Maybe it's a life free of anger, but you haven't found your way out. Or a life free of addiction, but you're banging against the window. That's what rebellion does—it keeps us trapped and separated from the life of freedom, joy, and peace that God intends for us.

What if you asked God to help you get free? I stood there, watching over that bird, wanting so badly to free him. If I felt that way toward a little bird, imagine how much more intensely God feels about us, His very own creation and children.

After several minutes watching this tiny creature struggle, I knew I needed to try to save him or he'd die. I must've seemed like a huge monster—and the little guy probably had never been touched by a human before, so he didn't know whether I'd crush him or help him. But I went in and opened the shade, and because he was so exhausted, his miniature body stopped struggling the moment I cupped my huge hands around him. This small hummingbird chose to trust me. And because he let me hold him, I could set him free.

If you've ever felt like that little bird—trapped by something, trying everything in your power to free yourself, but all your efforts have left you defeated and hopeless—did you know that God is ready to set you free? Try trusting Him. "It is for freedom that Christ has set us free" (Gal. 5:1). Let Him hold you so you can finally find freedom.

But as Paul emphasized, you have a role to play. Check your heart for any rebellious weeds; then pull them out—roots and all. God's plans are good, His ways are best, and His intention is not to harm you but to *set you free*. So weaken the spirit of rebellion and strengthen the spirit of obedience, and you'll begin to feel God's smile again.

## DISCUSSION QUESTIONS

1. When do you feel most attacked by Satan? Read 1 Peter 5:8–9. How can you actively and daily resist him?

2. Share about a time when you tried to rationalize or minimize your rebellion or outrun your conscience.

3. What would it look like for you to weaken the spirit of rebellion and strengthen the spirit of obedience?

# 10

# FEWER POSSESSIONS, MORE PEOPLE

When we moved twenty-eight years ago to White Bear Lake, Minnesota, my starting salary was $42,000 a year. We didn't have any debt, but we didn't have any money either. We were both thirty-four years old and had never owned a home, so we thought the time was right. We spent one day with a realtor looking at a dozen homes, and the last one we saw was the one we wanted. But it was $150,000, beyond anything we could afford. However, our realtor assured us we could make the mortgage payments if we lived frugally, so we bought the house and barely scraped by.

Those early years were very lean. Our cars were old, our family-room furniture was tattered and torn, and our living room had no furniture at all. We lived that way for several years, and every little expense became a point of contention. I specifically remember a major argument over a three-dollar potato peeler—the one we had was dysfunctional, but that was three dollars needed elsewhere. After a few years and a few modest raises, Laurie started saving up for living-room furniture by squirreling away birthday money, Christmas money, and anything she could get her hands on.

I grew up fishing with my dad and brother, so living just one mile away from one of the best fishing lakes in the Twin Cities? A dream. About once a week, I drove the kids down to the lake and waded while we fished for sunfish and bass. It was perfect. Watching Meg and Dave shriek with excitement as bass grabbed their bait and pulled on the ends of their lines gave me pure joy.

Until I wanted more.

I was thirty-six years old, lived a mile from the lake, and almost everyone I knew had a boat. So I began to believe a boat was the one thing that could make me happy. I floated the idea to Laurie. (Well, more like insisted, argued, and said that if you live in Minnesota, owning a boat is practically expected.) *Plus*, our deacon board's chairman had listed his boat for sale—an old fourteen-foot Lund fishing boat and trailer. The paint had worn off from thirty years of use, but it was perfect. Basically a sign from God.

But it was $900.

The money would have to come out of Laurie's furniture fund, but I reasoned, "What can you do with furniture except sit on it?" A great way to open the conversation.

For the two next hours, we argued. I used every persuasive maneuver in the book, and so did she, until we were both exhausted. Then I left to go play basketball. But I made it clear the debate wasn't over.

When I returned later that night, Laurie had already gone upstairs to bed. I turned on the television, and as I began to unwind, my mind returned to our argument. I replayed the conversation and began pondering what really mattered to me. And for one of the few times in my life, I decided to obey Ephesians 5:21: "Submit to one another out of reverence for Christ." So I did. I let it go. There would be other boats, and deep down I knew it wasn't the best time to spend our money on a boat anyway. The next day I told her my decision. If she wasn't comfortable with getting a boat right then, neither was I.

Three days later, I was at a board meeting with the guy selling the boat, and I shared with him what I'd decided. Empathetic, he said he understood.

Picture this—we live about a mile from church. I mindlessly drove home, turned into our neighborhood, and headed up the street. Suddenly, while still two blocks away from my house, I saw it in the driveway: a fourteen-foot Lund boat and trailer. With two huge red bows on it! I was stunned. Two days earlier, Laurie had purchased the boat from my chairman, who then arranged to have it dropped off during our meeting. So there I was, pulling into our driveway with my mouth agape. I exited the car and read the card on the boat. It simply said, "Happy anniversary. I love you. Laurie." The level of sacrifice Laurie showed in that gesture still moves me to this day.

During the next few years, the kids and I made such happy memories while fishing on White Bear Lake. One of David's friends, Luke, loved fishing—he lived for it. One evening Luke and Dave asked me to take them for a quick outing; Meg tagged along. On about the third cast, Luke hooked a monster. He stood on the front seat, his fishing pole bending, line zinging off his reel. All chaos erupted and Luke was in a panic. I yelled from the back of the boat, "Hang on, Luke! It's probably a big northern pike." Twenty minutes later, the fish began to tire, Luke gained ground, and from the deep water rose a forty-inch, twenty-pound muskie. When Meg saw it, she screamed and jumped up on her seat. To her it looked like a torpedo with razor-sharp teeth.

But *zing!* Down it went and disappeared into the deep, stripping line off Luke's reel for a final fight. When it rose a second time, I grabbed its enormous tail with one hand and cradled its huge body with my free arm. I remember lifting the large fish and holding it tightly across my lap—while all three kids stared with mouths wide open. Luke had just landed the biggest fish I'd ever seen caught, and nobody knew what to say. Luke spoke first, and his exact words were "If I died right now, I'd be a happy man." He was twelve. We released the great fish back into the water, and the four of us have a memory we'll take to our graves.

I loved my little fishing boat. But then I noticed my prize possession was beginning to possess me. For one, I got tired of finding places to store it. I kept it in a farmer's shed for a while, but every spring I spent half a day scrubbing off the dirt and bird droppings. Then I stored it in my garage, where it became a dumping place for tools, lawn chairs, turkey decoys—you name it. Furthermore, I made endless trips to the store to replace trailer lights and flat tires and spent half my life standing in line at the DMV to renew the plates and registration. Oh, and the motor. That ol' ten-horse Mercury was in the repair shop more times than I even used it. My beloved boat became a time-consuming, money-sucking, space-hogging beast.

There's a common saying among boat owners that I've found true: the happiest day of your life is when you get a boat; the second happiest day is when you sell it.

I asked a friend who lived on the lake whether I could put my boat for sale in his yard. I got a call the very next day, and a guy gave me $900 cash, hitched it to his truck, and drove off down the road. I'll never forget that moment. I watched my boat drive away, and instead of feeling an ounce of sadness, I said to myself, "There goes all my problems." The relief was glorious.

## POSSESSED BY POSSESSIONS

Is anything you possess actually beginning to possess *you*? Maybe a cabin, boat, snowmobile, ATV, RV, property, or time-share? You've spent a maddening amount of energy fixing it, storing it, and working overtime to pay for it …

There's absolutely nothing wrong with having any of these possessions. And many people who've been blessed with such resources are extremely generous about letting others enjoy them. Admittedly my wife and I own many nice things. We own our house, two cars, and, yes, furniture in the living room. I have enough hunting and fishing gear to stock a small store. And presently I have ten pairs of hunting boots, which is kind of my thing. Don't judge me: "God … richly provides us with everything for our enjoyment" (1 Tim. 6:17). A guy can never have enough boots.

But …

Jesus said, "Watch out! Be on your guard against all kinds of greed; life does not consist in an abundance of possessions" (Luke 12:15).

We want things to fulfill us and make us happy. But Jesus knew our possessions can't do what we want them to do. An inanimate object can never deliver the life we want.

Have you ever gotten something you wanted but still felt empty after you acquired it? That's because an object made of metal, wood, rubber, or porcelain can't encourage you, calm you, or soothe your heart's ache. You can love it, but it can't love you back. Even if you own a Harley and you store it in your living room during the winter, where you can look at it, polish it, and picture how good you look on it, it'll never love you back.

However, we go from one purchase to the next because acquiring something new provides an immediate high. But then each new item sits somewhere unused and that high wears off. Wouldn't you say that's generally true? Most of the stuff we have in our basements, on our garage shelves, or in storage units seldom gets used. I bought a dozen goose decoys twenty years ago, and guess what? They're still in the box unopened. More importantly, they're incapable of loving me or reducing the anxiety that I harbor deep within. Same with my boots, bikes, deck, or phone.

Again, there's nothing wrong with having wealth, equipment, furniture, boats, or assets. We all have and need certain possessions to live in this world. The actual property owned isn't wrong; it's what we think it will do for us—make us happy and whole—that's wrong. That's when we risk missing the new life God has planned for us.

While I love my home, yard, and French press and while I'm attracted to nice things as much as anyone, we have to be done with the value we place on them—because they'll never be enough.

# IT'S NOT WHAT BUT WHO

It's easy to buy into the lie that how much we acquire matters most in life—how big of a house we can build, the kind of car we drive, and the number that appears on our retirement account. If it's up, we're up; if it drops, we drop. Pointless, isn't it? It can be just a number on a screen or a piece of paper, but we let things like this dictate our emotions and consume our minds.

Author Brant Hansen wrote, "The lie, for most of us, is that we'll 'get there,' that we'll somehow, someday, make it to a point where that thing, that whatever, that we think we need to be secure, is finally ours, and we won't be threatened anymore, because we made it. But there is no 'there.'"[1]

If we fall for that lie, we'll miss the new life of love, joy, and peace. Because Jesus was clear—the abundant life does not consist in an abundance of *things* (see Luke 12:15). Solomon, the extremely wealthy and wise king, even said, "Whoever loves money never has enough" (Eccl. 5:10). Let me emphasize, money isn't bad; we all need a certain amount to live in this world. But it's the *love* of it—the obsession with it—God warns us about. Instead, He tells us to be done with our love for money because it'll never satisfy and we'll never be happy with what we have. "This is the day that the Lord has made. Let us be full of joy and be glad in it" (Ps. 118:24 NLV). Not tomorrow, not next week, not even five years from now—but *this* day. Let us rejoice in the little joys and pleasures of *this* day.

I'm not saying I have this mastered—because I don't. But thankfully my possessions are losing their hold on me. I'm finding more and more that what really matters in life is not what but *who*. People always matter to Jesus, and they should matter to us too—more than our belongings, our image, our hunting gear, and our money all combined. This tension between loving my possessions and loving people is constant. What about you? Too often we love our things and use people—but it should be the opposite. We should love people and use our things.

We'd probably all agree that should be the case, especially when a wave of loneliness hits. I've been there; you have too. You lost a job, your group of friends abandoned you, you had a major fight with your spouse or kids, or someone packed his or her bags and left you. And nothing—not your house, car, music, dog, or even your church—could take away the pain in your heart.

What do you do when you *want* to love people but no one close is left to be found?

Last week I received an email from a gal in her late twenties:

> While listening to one of your messages during break at work, I welled up in tears at my desk (thankfully, my coworkers didn't notice). When you confessed to struggling in life with very few friends, it rang so true for me. I look around, and everybody else has a best friend or several close friends. My parents are very supportive, but they are the only people I can really talk to.
>
> I'm not a partier, so I was left out of a lot of things in high school, college, and even now because it seems like that's all people care about. I joined the Y and volunteer at church, but so far, I haven't made any close friends from either of those.

Most of us feel a void like this, don't we? At some point in our lives, we've been there, and believe it or not, even the partiers feel as if they're on the outside looking in. But God made us for friendship—with Himself first and then with others. So when those two kinds of friendship are missing or lacking, a void is left in our hearts that nothing but love from God and others can fill.

Just two days ago, as my wife and I walked our dog, we happened to choose a random route that took us past the home of our friends Tony and Diane. They were out in their yard doing some work, so we stopped under the shade of their huge maple tree and chatted a bit. Then Laurie paired off with Diane, and Tony came by me, and it was really nice. Nothing big, no great new insights about life—just an update on the kids and grandkids. But that little connection with those friends soothed something in my soul.

When we continued our walk, I said to Laurie, "Tony and Diane are the nicest people. I wonder if they'd welcome us into their small group of friends so we could pray for and support each other." Laurie loved the idea, and we quietly vowed to explore that—in two years. See, that's the problem. It's never the right time—we're too busy, it's not convenient, or we have other obligations to meet first.

But I'm growing. At this point in my life, I'm finally seeing the pathway out of the old life of emptiness and into the newer life of wholeness by shifting affections away from possessions and more toward people. Here's how.

## CONFRONT YOUR NAKED TRUTH

At some point you have to get brutally honest about your naked-ness. (My editor urged me for a better word than *nakedness*, like *vulnerability*, but stay with me.) Job said, "Naked I came from my mother's womb, and naked I will depart" (1:21). As he observed, there's not a single thing you and I possess that will last; everything we have will stay here. We came into the world naked, we'll leave naked, and all the days in between, we're still pretty naked.

Oh, we cover our nakedness with various styles and colors of clothes. We transport our nakedness in different types of cars and trucks. We house our nakedness with varying sizes of rooms and furnishings. We exercise it on treadmills and in yoga classes. We feed it, medicate it, and tuck it into bed at night. But no matter what we wear or drive or what kind of house we walk into each evening, underneath it all is just a person who came with nothing and will leave with nothing—just like every other person on the planet.

Being aware of our total destitution should help us hold on to things loosely. Because if we realize our houses, cars, physical beauty, and retirement funds are not actually ours for the taking, there's less reason to stress so much over them.

The life expectancy in the United States for a man my age is eighty-one years old, and that number should inform me how to live.[2] Remembering my days on earth are short focuses me on what's really important—it's sitting on the floor with my grandkids, enjoying walks with my wife, celebrating milestones with my kids, and deepening my relationship with God. Knowing I'm probably going to die in the next twenty years helps me stop comparing myself with people who have more possessions than me. Because quite simply—those who have a lot just have a lot more to leave and lose. Jesus told us to avoid the mistake of gaining the world but losing our souls (see Matt. 16:26). That'd be a really bad deal, wouldn't it? To pile up possessions for eighty-one years on earth, only to lose your soul for eighty-one billion years of eternal darkness and isolation? Not a good trade-off.

If we don't confront the naked truth, we'll spend too much time and money on things that remain here on earth and not enough on the one thing that goes with us. Because ultimately the only thing you take with you into heaven is other people. And when that truth sinks in, you begin to shift from loving possessions to loving people. And you dip your toes into a newer, freer kind of life.

## GIVE MORE THAN YOU TAKE

Author and pastor Erwin McManus wrote, "The most basic definition I've used for wholeness is simply 51 percent. You know, where you give more than you take.... What if in every situation you made a commitment to make a greater contribution than withdrawal— whether financial, relational, emotional, or the investment of your time?"[3] McManus recounted how Jesus provided the perfect example of wholeness. He didn't give just 51 percent either; He gave 100 percent of Himself. He showed us the pathway to new life, life we find when we become givers not takers. McManus said, "As contrary as it may seem, the person who gives away the most of himself will have the greatest experience of love. The depth and profound nature of love can only be known in the context of personal sacrifice for others. This is why wholeness comes only in the act of giving rather than the pursuit of getting. We are most whole when we are most free to give."[4]

In Mark 12 a religious leader asked Jesus what it all came down to: "Of all the commandments, which is the most important?"

(v. 28). Jesus told him the two most important commandments: "Love the Lord your God with all your heart and with all your soul and with all your mind … [and] love your neighbor as yourself" (vv. 30–31). Get those right, and you'll get life right. Love God, and love others.

While the greatest commandments directly address relationships, the Ten Commandments are about relationships too. McManus suggested that a summary of the last six commandments could be "Don't be a taker": "The fifth calls us to not live as takers in relationship to our parents, but to honor them; the sixth tells us not to take someone else's life; the seventh commands us to not take another person's spouse; the eighth, not to take one's possessions; the ninth, not to take someone's good reputation; and the tenth, not to *want* to take what is our neighbor's."[5]

What would it look like if you gave more than you took? What kindness could you give to your spouse, child, friend, or coworker? What sacrifice of time could you offer? What compliment or word of encouragement could you impart? Now, this all implies you have something *to give*, because you can't give what you don't have. So if you're in a downward spiral of self-loathing and neediness, you won't be able to offer any sort of gift or genuine kindness to others.

And that leads to the third way of shifting your affections away from possessions and toward people.

## EMBRACE YOUR BROKENNESS

One of my board members and very good friends once said to me, "Bob, you're actually at your best when you're in a weakened state."

What? We've been through a lot together, and he's seen me through my highest highs and lowest lows. So I just looked at him and tried to make sense of it.

Let me be clear—I don't like to feel weak, and I work hard at being strong and on top of my game. And when the chips are down, I especially think it's important for a leader to put on a strong front to lift the troops and set the tone. So what did my friend mean by saying that I'm best when I'm weak?

Paul offered some insights, because he expressed this concept long before my friend did. Paul said, "When I am weak, then I am strong" (2 Cor. 12:10). When Paul was weakened, exposed, and vulnerable, he was able to find strength. How? Paul knew that when we are weak, we're more likely to humble ourselves and turn to God, and when we're broken, frail, or desperate, His power shows up best. Because in those moments He clearly gets the credit. If we cry out to God and ask Him to touch the deepest corners of our broken and lonely hearts, He will heal us—not by our power but by His.

We don't like to be broken, and we work hard at maintaining the façade that we have it all together. But if we're honest, part of what life does is break us. We get betrayed, hurt, stepped on, and shut out. We suffer heartaches and losses. And some days it feels a lot like despair.

But what if those dark holes of loneliness and despair are blessings? What if they force us back to Jesus, who urged, "Come to me, all you who are weary and burdened" (Matt. 11:28)? What if the hard times are opportunities for us to recognize that we actually aren't self-sufficient and, if we try to go through life without Jesus, we'll lose? What if our seasons of weakness, loneliness, and fear help us empathize with others—who surely are also feeling weak, alone, and afraid?

Maybe during this time of brokenness, God wants to teach us about relying on Him for our wholeness instead of relying on our yoga instructor. And maybe what God wants to deepen and develop *in* us is more important than what He wants to do *through* us. Maybe there's a relationship pattern or character flaw God is addressing so it won't be a tripping point in the friendships He wants to bring into our lives. I think God wants us to learn to trust Him more than anything—and I don't do that very well when I'm feeling strong and self-sufficient.

Will you trust Jesus? Really trust Him, especially during the hard times? Will you go to Him, ask Him to heal you and do for you what nobody else can? Will you allow Him to make you whole, happy, and ready for new and lasting friends?

## LOOK CLOSER TO HOME

When it comes to finding friends, why do we sometimes think there will be someone better out there in another city or state? Your potential new best friends are not living in Toledo (unless you live in Toledo). Don't look past the people God has put right in front of you. Your best friendship opportunities are in *your proximity*— where you work, live, go to school, and attend church. And it's not many but a few you're seeking—your spouse, kids, grandkids, and a few friends.

Author John Ortberg mentioned a statistic that Darren Hardy included in his book *The Entrepeneur Roller Coaster*: about ten people cry at the average funeral.[6] So who are the ten or so people who'll cry at your funeral? I made a list: my wife, daughter, son, and their spouses make it to the top. My mom would, but she's eighty-seven—so what are the odds? My brother and three sisters probably, but I'm sure one or two of their spouses would say, "Oh, well ..." Then there'd be a few close friends, and that'd be about it.

Now, here's the question: Am I giving the best of my time and life to the ones who will cry at my funeral?

Too often I give my best to people I don't know and who don't really care about me. So in recent years I've been declining golf invitations and social outings so I can give my best to those people who really matter to me. Jesus did this well. He had twelve friends, and of those twelve, He spent most of His time with three: Peter, James, and John. The most perfect model of humanity had only three close friends, which means He must've disappointed a lot of people who wanted His time. We must learn to disappoint some people too and be okay with it.

## THE INNER CIRCLE

If I sketched it out, the people who really matter to me fall into three small circles: family, work, and friends—and even then, only a few people make it into each circle. These three smaller circles are set inside one ultimate circle. In the example below, you'll notice old college friends, social media followers, acquaintances, and relatives fall outside this larger circle.

## LAW OF THE INNER CIRCLE

RELATIVES

OLD COLLEGE
FRIENDS

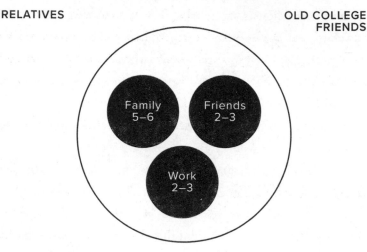

Family
5–6

Friends
2–3

Work
2–3

SOCIAL MEDIA
FOLLOWERS

ACQUAINTANCES

When I identify those inside the ultimate circle, I know who gets my primary yes. I also know who gets my primary no—just about everyone else outside the circle. Learn to disappoint.

Also, lifelong friendships are very rare. More commonly friendships change based on proximity, interests, and stage of life. It doesn't mean you don't care about or pray for those outside the circle; it just means those relationships get less of us.

Ultimately, my life and yours will be measured not by how many acquaintances we have or what we possessed or accomplished but by how we gave ourselves to those who really matter to us.

Shauna Niequist maintained a running tally of trips, conferences, airports visited, and talks she had prepared for the masses. But it left her feeling exhausted. She wrote, "Let me tell you where [love's] not:

it's not in numbers—numbers in bank accounts, numbers on scales, numbers on report cards or credit scores. The love you're looking for is never something you can calculate." She also observed, "Here's the love: it's in marriage and parenting. It's in family and friends. It's in sacrifice and forgiveness. It's in dinner around the coffee table and long walks. It's in the hands and faces of the people we see every day, in the whispers of our prayers and hymns and songs."[7]

And love will always require intentionality, sacrifice, and forgiveness.

## ISLA MUJERES

A few years ago Laurie and I made big plans to take our kids and their spouses on a one-week vacation to Isla Mujeres, Mexico. We'd never done anything like that before, and we wanted to invest in our family before grandkids came along and life got nuts. Our son-in-law also had a short window before he started residency at the Mayo Clinic, so it was now or never. We made our plans, booked the flights, and paid a small fortune to rent a house on a rocky cliff overlooking the turquoise-blue water of the Caribbean Sea.

The trip started rough. The day we left Minneapolis, everyone was under a lot of stress. A couple of us were crying as we boarded the plane, and we all got a little seasick on the ferry ride over to the island. But I prayed God would do something special in our family, bring the six of us together in a deeper way, and build a lasting memory.

I need to say this carefully (and he has given me permission), but my son-in-law, Nelly, had a difficult upbringing. His parents divorced when he was one. Raised by a single mom who worked full time, he was alone a lot. He saw little of his dad, who was often absent and disengaged. And I know well how this kind of home life affects little kids. Author John Eldredge called it a *father wound*, which makes every child wonder, *Does my dad love me? Does he think I'm strong, pretty, or talented? Does he think I have what it takes?*[8] And when a father is absent or immoral, those questions never get answered and feelings of insecurity and low self-confidence are magnified.

So I decided long ago I'd be a father to Nelly—not replace his dad but just be a loving father figure to him. I've tried to do that in big and small ways—like taking him fishing and hunting and teaching him how to change the oil in his car and replace broken side mirrors. And I make a point to encourage him, hug him, and tell him how proud of him I am.

By day two on our trip, the warm Mexican sun and lazy pace began to seep into our souls. A spirit of playfulness surrounded the pool, and friendly banter filled our morning walks up and down the rocky coastline. Our only mode of transportation was a four-seat golf cart, and we experienced the island shops, restaurants, and people up close. Each day was a new tropical gift.

On the fourth night, the six of us crammed onto that golf cart, and it tilted badly to one side. But it didn't matter—we took off with laughter and more banter and parked in front of a very modest-looking establishment.

The gals were dressed in sundresses and flip-flops; the guys, in nice shorts and golf shirts. The host led us back to an open-air dining area enclosed by high stone walls and nicely decorated with plants and trees. Turns out the owner was also the chef, and it became apparent he was going to do the whole thing—from serving us to cooking on the grill. It seemed as if it was all planned just for us, and since we were the only ones there, it felt very intimate.

So I decided to take a risk. "We don't have to do this, and if you think it's dorky or stupid, we won't. But what if each of us thought of one thing we were thankful for this past year and just shared it."

Meg started off, and David's wife, Sara, jumped in. Both offered great responses.

Then it was Dave's turn. He looked at Meg and Nelly, who had been through a lot in their young marriage. In the beginning Nelly was wait-listed to a couple of medical schools in the United States, so rather than waiting for a slot, he opted for the one opportunity that was immediately open to him: Ross University School of Medicine on the island of Dominica. Not Dominican Republic; that would've been easy. But Dominica is an impoverished Caribbean island that you've never heard of—and it was brutal. For two years he and my daughter lived in isolation and poverty. It also wasn't safe; more than once Meg called home in tears, hoping she could go home after being harassed on the two-hour bus ride to the only grocery store available. And after two years in Dominica, they moved to Saginaw, Michigan, to finish Nelly's third year of medical school. Really, they barely held on.

So that night in Mexico, my son turned toward his sister and brother-in-law and with tenderness said, "I am so proud of you guys. You've been through so much—no money, living in crappy apartments far from family, wondering if you'd make it. But here you are. Nelly, Sara and I are so thankful you're in our family." I felt my eyes fill up, and the tears flowed.

Then it was Nelly's turn.

The table grew quiet, and he couldn't speak while tears rolled down his face. But he finally managed to say, "What I'm thankful for is this family, *because I know I belong*. You have no idea how much this family means to me, and to be a part of it is beyond anything I could express."

Oh man. At that point there wasn't a dry eye at our table. I don't know what else God was doing in the universe that night, but it seemed as if He put everything aside and shone His love down on that little table in No-where's-ville, Mexico, and said, "Just take it in. Take in My love. Take in one another's love because this is what heaven's like. This is the life I intend for you to have."

Not just me—that's the life God intends for *all of us*. Every human heart cries out for belonging, and maybe you feel as if you don't belong. Maybe you feel alone, abandoned, unnoticed, or unloved. But God says that through Jesus you belong to Him and you belong to this family of believers. When you get that right, you can get life right. It's not about loving possessions; we can be done with that pursuit. It's about loving God and taking steps to love the ones God gives you.

## DISCUSSION QUESTIONS

1. Is there anything you possess that's begun to possess you?
2. In what ways can you give more than you take in your relationships with your spouse, family, and friends?
3. Create a list of the people who really matter to you. Who are the ten who will cry at your funeral, and is there anything you need to change to make sure those ten are getting your best?

# LESS SELFISHNESS, MORE SACRIFICE

I hate to admit this, and it's one of the ugliest things about me, but I'm selfish. It's unnatural for me to think of others first (or even think about them at all), and my knee-jerk response to almost everything is to care for myself, protect myself, entertain myself, and make myself more comfortable and prosperous. But nowhere does the Bible tell us to pursue comfort or elevate ourselves above others. It says things like "Take up your cross, and follow me" (Matt. 16:24 NLT) and "Offer your bodies as a living sacrifice" (Rom. 12:1) and "Give yourself up, as Christ gave Himself up" (see Eph. 5:25). Scripture calls us to crosses and sacrifices, but crosses and sacrifices tend to be where things die. I don't like that. I'd like to avoid that.

Three summers ago my daughter and son-in-law were moving from Rochester, Minnesota, to Columbia, Missouri, to continue Nelly's residency. So they rented a truck, and my wife—who tends to be overly generous—said, "The kids need a grill, so let's give them ours."

I responded naturally: "Let 'em get their *own* grill."

She said, "We need a new one anyway. Let's just give them ours."

"We *wouldn't* need a new one if we kept the old one," I protested.

Sure, the wheels were missing, and parts were rusted off, but it worked fine. Then I actually wondered, *What would Jesus do if He had a grill? Jesus probably didn't even have a grill. So if He didn't have a grill, why do our kids need a grill?* Finally I gave in, and there went my perfectly good grill onto their truck.

But apparently my generosity didn't need to end there. Laurie came at me again, this time saying, "They need a bed for their guest room, so I'm gonna give them the one in our guest room."

"We're not giving them our bed!" I insisted.

"We need a new one in there anyway."

"What's wrong with it?" I asked.

"It's more than thirty years old, and it sags."

"But nobody sleeps in it."

She said, "My parents are coming in three weeks, and we'll need a new bed."

I said, "We're not getting a new bed just for your parents. They're eighty-five, and they're used to saggy things."

But off we went to a mattress store to buy a new one, and onto the truck went our old bed. Mysteriously, our lawn mower and my favorite rocking chair also wound up on the truck, and it wasn't until we unloaded in Missouri that I realized they'd been hijacked.

"Hey, that's my favorite rocking chair!" I blurted out. To which Laurie said, "You never use it." To which I said, "I *might* use it if we brought it up from the basement."

So now, whenever we visit the kids in Missouri, we grill burgers on my perfectly good grill, sleep in my perfectly good bed, mow their lawn with my perfectly good mower, and rock the baby in my perfectly good rocker.

The point is—I'm not good about letting others have my stuff, because I'm fundamentally selfish. I mean, people should get their own stuff—isn't that how life is supposed to work?

When Blue was a puppy, he'd yelp to go out every morning at 5:00. It was dark and cold out, so when Laurie and I heard his first bark, neither of us wanted to move. We were sleepy and warm, and that moment tested my selfishness every morning. Who would make the first move? Which of us was so loving, so sacrificial, so much like Jesus that when the dog whined, that person would get up and let him out? At 5:00 a.m. I'm none of those things. Rather, my mind said, *Don't move, breathe, or twitch. If you lie here for ten seconds, she'll get up.* Admittedly, on opening day of deer season, I spring out of bed at 5:00 a.m. But when the dog yelped, there was no springing. Because I'm selfish.

The ugliness comes out the most not when Blue barks at 5:00 a.m. but whenever I travel. As I'm boarding a plane, one of my first concerns is, *Will I be able to establish armrest dominance?* Once, on a flight from Fairbanks to Minneapolis, my seatmate arrived before me. He'd already established armrest dominance, and he wasn't relenting. It irked me. I thought, *Doesn't he know I'm here and want my fair share of the armrest? How presumptuous. How rude.*

But then a wonderful thing happened. Two hours into the flight, he had to get up to use the restroom. This provided the perfect opportunity, and you'd better believe I took over the armrest. I totally hogged it, and what's more—I secretly enjoyed watching him squirm when he got back. *Deal with it. Fair is fair. That's how life is supposed to work.*

Isn't it amazing what selfishness does? Instead of chatting with this guy or caring anything about his soul's condition (or even his elbow's), I was concerned about one thing: armrest dominance. Was I happier because I got it? A little. But what if I had let it go from the beginning and enjoyed those first two hours of the flight? What if I could've been loving and selfless? (After I told this story in church, someone who works in the airline industry dropped off an actual commercial airline armrest with a big red bow on it.)

First Corinthians 13:5 says, "[Love] does not demand its own way" (NLT). Whenever I demand my own way and hog the armrest, I'm unable to love others. Because it's all about what *I* want, what *I* demand, what *I* think is fair. And when it's all about me, it can never be about loving you.

That's why selfishness is nothing but a relationship killer; a relationship requires two people, but when it's only about me, it can never be about somebody else.

Selfishness isn't just our personal problem; it's the god of our culture too. We live in a self-centered culture. So much so that the word *selfie* won the 2013 word of the year from Oxford Dictionaries,[1] and in 2015 more people died taking selfies than from shark attacks.[2] And while the average life span is about 27,000 days, millennials are on pace to take 25,000 selfies (per person in his or her lifetime)—which means each person averages almost one selfie per day in the course of his or her life.[3] That's not counting the average hours per week spent editing these selfies for better clarity, color, and poses. (We baby boomers would do it too—except most of us don't know how.)

One journalist observed, "Selfies have by now become an epidemic,"[4] and it's true—we're obsessed with ourselves. David Foster Wallace captured the fact that we're chronically self-centered in the commencement address he delivered at Kenyon College in 2005: "Everything in my own immediate experience supports my deep belief that I am the absolute center of the universe, the realest, most vivid and important person in existence.... Think about it: there is no experience you've had that you were not at the absolute center of. The world as you experience it is there in front of you, or behind you, to the left or right of you."[5]

When you're the center of your universe, you end up with a big dose of *you*. But that makes for a lonely life. You get self-love, but you don't get real love. You get what you want, but you tend to lose your way. And you end up forfeiting all the things you crave most, like true friendship and belonging. The biggest reason people feel isolated is that they're always at the center of their selfies—and their lives—and certain places in the human soul can't be filled by a big dose of you. Even if you edit and enhance the best version of yourself, it's still not what your soul longs for.

I will always struggle with selfishness, but I'm learning how firmly it keeps me stuck in the old life. It shows up in my anger toward those who hog the armrest, in my entitlement when I'm the center of my universe, in my greed because it's all about me, and in my loneliness—because who wants to be around a self-centered jerk who won't share? It's been a long, slow turn, but I'm starting to shift from selfishness to sacrifice.

The same man who said "The old [life] has gone, the new [life] is here" (2 Cor. 5:17) also wrote, "I urge you, brothers and sisters, in view of God's mercy, to offer your bodies as a living sacrifice, holy and pleasing to God—this is your true and proper worship. Do not conform to the pattern of this world, but be transformed by the renewing of your mind. Then you will be able to test and approve what God's will is—his good, pleasing and perfect will" (Rom. 12:1–2).

Paul explained that the transformation from the old life to the new comes when we offer our bodies as living sacrifices. Sacrifice is the opposite of selfishness—because if I sacrifice something, I'm giving up something I value.

In the Old Testament, a sacrifice usually involved an animal's death. In that agrarian culture, sheep and cattle were the people's lifeblood, so when God instructed His people to sacrifice an animal without blemish, they were giving up something of great value (see Deut. 17:1). Why did God ask them to do this? So they'd remember to keep Him at the center of their lives and not themselves. God of course knew all about the sin of self-centeredness and how it not only creates strife in relationships but causes His people to drift further from Him as well.

God doesn't want a dead sacrifice from us, however, but specifically instructs, "Offer your bodies as a *living* sacrifice." He asks us to relinquish things we value *while we're alive* instead of being forced to relinquish them the day we die. Wills are great, but it's not a sacrifice to give away everything when you're dead. Because at that point, who cares? And it's not as if you did it willingly either. It's a sacrifice only if you give away something valued while you're alive, and surely that costs you something.

But here's the twist: in order to offer your body as a living sacrifice, *something* has to die. Selfishness has to die. Greed has to die. Fear of losing something you value has to die. Your own comfort sometimes has to die.

*Well, that's not fun.*

What does every American want? Fun!

*What is fun? What is valuable?*

The goal of every Friday night is to have fun. Even when a kid goes to a party or event, the first thing a parent asks when that child gets home is "Was it fun?" Not "Was it challenging, inspiring, or sacrificial?" That would be weird. But "Was it *fun?*"

Even in our relationships, our entertainment, and the food we prepare for dinner, that's the goal. All that matters is whether we enjoyed ourselves. That's why the HGTV dream exists—go beach-front-bargain hunting so we can escape any sort of conflict, work, or challenge, and live out our days in a hammock. We work and live for fun.

So all this talk of sacrifice and giving up something is completely irrational. It's not fun, and it certainly isn't American.

But God doesn't call us to lives of fun or even comfort. These things aren't bad, but they aren't the endgame. Rather, God calls us to lives of sacrifice, of taking up our crosses daily, and of following Him (see Matt. 16:24). This is what Paul said leads to the life we all crave deep inside. Sacrifice is not always fun or entertaining, but it's fulfilling. It's purposeful. It builds marriages, mends families, forges friendships, and offsets evil in the world. A hammock can't do those things. But when you surrender something you value for the sake of another, you can change someone's life ... and often you get love in return.

In his book *The End of Me*, Kyle Idleman wrote, "To live [real life] you have to die first.... The end of me is where real life begins."[6] Strange words that hold eternal truth.

"You died, and your life is now hidden with Christ" (Col. 3:3). There is a dying that leads to living and a giving up that leads to rising up. "Just as Christ was raised from the dead ... we too may live a new life" (Rom. 6:4). How do we make the shift from selfishness to sacrifice? Three concepts found in Scripture provide the key.

# DIE DAILY

*Make good choices*

Jesus said, "Take up [your] cross *daily* and follow me" (Luke 9:23). A cross is an instrument of death, and selfishness is so strong in us we have to confront and crucify it every day. Often we choose whether we will do this or not in the little things. Who's going to get up with the baby? Who's going to load the dishwasher, take out the trash, fix dinner, and give up the armrest?

One of our pastors, Don Graffam, said, "At our house it's the battle of the S.O.S. pad. My morning ritual is to put an egg in a bowl, microwave it for twenty-two seconds, put it on an English muffin, and have an Egg McGraffam." But for years Don left the bowl in the sink, and the resulting crusted residue made it hard to clean.

This grew into a major battle for the Graffams, and it resumed every morning—until Don decided to pick up the scrubber and clean it himself. But Don shared with me the ultimate truth for us all: "As small as it sounds, the battle of the S.O.S. is everything. If you don't figure that out quickly and learn to die to selfishness daily in the little things, your marriage will die a slow death."

Kyle Idleman put it this way: "The problem with dying to myself is that it's so daily. I have to make the choice over and over again. I can live for myself or I can live for Christ, which means picking up my cross—at the drugstore, at the gas pump, in my living room, in traffic."[7] The battle between selfishness and sacrifice often shows up in the little stuff. Where do you need to make the sacrifice, pick up the S.O.S., and clean out the bowl?

# SACRIFICE OUT OF FULLNESS

You can't be a living sacrifice if you have nothing to sacrifice, and you can't give what you don't have. God gave us all something we can sacrifice. For some of us, that might be time or talents rather than something material. Others of us have been blessed materially. Either way, Jesus said, "From everyone who has been given much, much will be demanded" (Luke 12:48). That implies that some of us may have received little; others have been given much. (If you own a car, you fall into the category of those who've been given much. If you own two cars, you're *extremely* wealthy. And if you own two cars, a boat, and a storage unit full of stuff, you're *obscenely* wealthy. If you have no car but have abilities you can use to serve a neighbor, you've also been given much.) From the one to whom much is given, much is required.

The reason my daughter and son-in-law could take all my stuff is that I had stuff my wife was happy to give to them.

Have you ever heard the story of the prodigal son (if not, see Luke 15:11–32)? Of all the parables Jesus told, the parable of the lost son is the centerpiece. Most people focus on how the boy demanded his share of his father's estate, left home in rebellion, and squandered his money on "wild living" (v. 13). Later, he returned home and begged for his father's forgiveness. The story depicts God's willingness to forgive us no matter what we've done or how far we've wandered.

But what people often overlook in this famous story is that the father was very wealthy. His estate included hired servants. It wasn't a modest house with a few chickens; it was a vast parcel of land that required servants to make meals and care for the property.

When the boy returned home, the father draped a robe on his son's shoulders and slipped a ring on his finger—both symbols of wealth. Then he threw a grand feast with the finest wine and choicest cuts of beef to celebrate. Most of all, the father had stored up a wealth of love and forgiveness for his son, and he gave it freely from a full heart.

The father's giving heart is easier to imitate when we enjoy abundance in a given area. But you can't give what you don't have. For some people the idea of being sacrificial with one's money, possessions, time, or even love is defeating because they're bankrupt in one or more of those areas. Sometimes they're so depleted that they're just surviving.

If you've never been loved, it's hard to extend love. If you've never been forgiven, it's hard to forgive others. If you're in a perpetual state of deficiency, exhaustion, and neediness, it's difficult to be sacrificial. When you have nothing or little to give, selfishness becomes a way of life just to survive.

If this is you, there's hope. Come home to the Father. He lives in a mansion, He has a robe and ring, and He's waiting every day for you. Nobody is beyond the reach of His love, forgiveness, and healing. He has an unlimited supply of everything you need. All you have to do is receive His love; then you can give love. Receive His healing; then you can help others heal.

It's okay to receive for a while. There have been at least four seasons in my life when I was so depleted and desperate for God's healing that all I could do was receive, and a good counselor was a lifesaver during each of those seasons. But the goal is to be made whole again—to fill the depleted areas, heal the deep wounds, and restore the broken parts of the heart. Your knowledge and intellect can't heal your brokenness; only God can do that. So ask Him to fill, heal, and restore you so you can become a "living sacrifice, holy and pleasing to God" (Rom. 12:1). It's time to be done with the endless cycle of selfishness and self-preservation so you can be transformed and experience a newer and better life.

# WELCOME THE FIRE

"There is wonderful joy ahead, even though you must endure many trials for a little while. These trials will show that your faith is genuine. It is being tested as fire tests and purifies gold" (1 Pet. 1:6–7 NLT).

Fire purifies gold, and that fire must be severe enough to melt the gold into liquid, exposing and extracting the impurities. Did you know God will allow you to go through fiery trials so He can purify your faith and life?

Sometimes an impurity in our lives prevents us from living the new life God intends for us. And certain impurities are so stubborn that only a fire hot enough to melt metal can burn them away. So in loving-kindness God permits fiery trials to enter our lives—in hope that selfishness, arrogance, anger, sloth, or lust will be burned away. As hard as these tests may be, we can hold on because we know they're for our good. God gives us this promise about reaching the other side of the fire: "There is wonderful joy ahead."

In the summer of 2012, Colorado experienced severe drought, and on June 26 the temperature reached 101 degrees Fahrenheit with dry winds gusting to sixty-five miles an hour. These erratic winds fanned a wildfire into the infamous Waldo Canyon Fire. That fire became so destructive that it jumped containment lines and destroyed 18,247 acres and 346 homes.[8]

When this fire swept over the mountains, it headed for the home of John and Stasi Eldredge, and only an act of God would save their house. Friends were called, prayers were raised, and by what can be described only as God's sovereign protection, their home was spared. Everything behind their property—every tree, shrub, and grassy patch—was scorched and blackened with ash. But they remained safe.

In his book *Moving Mountains*, John wrote these wonderful words of discovery:

> The land was stripped bare. Even rocks were broken open from the furnace-heat of the fire. When I returned from wandering in a dead world, my shoes and socks were black with ash. I stopped taking those walks after a while; I had had enough with death and destruction....
>
> It was the following summer when I returned to the hills, reluctantly. It seemed way too much to hope that summer might bring with it a different message. When I crested the slope above our house, I was literally stopped in my tracks by what I saw. Wildflowers were blooming here, there, *everywhere*—happy little lavender asters, absurdly tall and joyful sunflowers, blood-red Indian paintbrush, clusters of purple penstemon. In greater abundance than I had ever seen before. The deep-rooted yuccas had survived and were shooting up with vigor, as was all the scrub oak. The wild grasses had grown waist high, swaying like a green sea in

the light breezes. Someone had washed the land with so much color and life it looked like a Van Gogh painting.[9]

Here is a profound truth: there's always growth after a fire.

I wish it were different. I wish every day were perfect and pleasant and we didn't need the fire. I wish my marriage was free of conflict and happy all the time. I wish I could have spared my kids from all the challenges we've been through. I wish my dad hadn't died. I wish my mom didn't have to live alone. I wish there wasn't heartbreak, sickness, infertility, miscarriage, or divorce. To quote Judith Viorst, "If I were in charge of the world / You wouldn't have lonely."[10] But we do have lonely, and nobody escapes the fire.

Nobody.

But we can have hope because growth will always follow the fire. God is faithful to take something meant for destruction and turn it into something good and refining. He may let a fiery trial sweep through our lives to remove something impure. And He may allow a blazing fire to barrel our way so something new and better can replace the old.

While you're walking through the scorching flames, you can feel hopeless and desperate. It's tough to breathe, because the smoke of fear envelops you. And some fires leave scars. Although they'll heal, they'll also leave a tender spot on your soul.

But growth will *always* come. When the smoke clears and the spring rains fall on our dry souls, we'll find God was there. And after the fire He will begin to fill our lives with things we never knew about. Tender shoots of empathy replace a hard heart. Lush grasses of intimacy replace a brittle marriage. Deep roots of trust replace a shallow faith in God. We discover a new and vibrant abundance from which we can give. And a colorful field of sacrifice will hopefully replace the ugly landscape of selfishness.

New growth.

New life.

A faithful God.

# DISCUSSION QUESTIONS

1. What do you tend to be most selfish about? How can you shift from being selfish to being sacrificial?

2. Go online and check out the Global Rich List. (You can simply search for that term.) How does knowing where you stand financially in comparison with the rest of the world change the way you view your own situation?

3. Jesus said in Luke 12:48, "From everyone who has been given much, much will be demanded." How are you being faithful with the resources God has given you?

12

# LESS OBSESSION, MORE DEVOTION

Early in our marriage Laurie and I were somewhat obsessed with antiques. We grew up in western Pennsylvania near the little hamlets of Volant, Slippery Rock, and New Wilmington (which was Amish country), and whenever we passed a horse and buggy on the side of the road, it was like seeing a snapshot of what life was like 150 years ago. Though I'd never want to travel exclusively in a horse and buggy or read by oil lanterns, the Amish life of simplicity and tranquility appeals to me. Maybe that's why we fell in love with antiques; there's something about a 130-year-old hand-crafted maple corner hutch or a pine dresser with wooden knobs or a heavy round oak pedestal table. They connect us to a time when life seemed more earthy and solid.

So when *American Pickers* first aired on the History Channel, I couldn't get enough of it. I loved watching Mike and Frank travel the country, knocking on the doors of old farms and junkyards, searching for stuff to buy. What artifact would they discover buried under layers of dust and debris? What treasure would they find in a backwoods pole barn that hadn't seen the light of day in decades?

One of Mike's favorite things was unearthing old bicycles under a junk pile in someone's rickety shed. One time he pulled out a rusty bike that had broken spokes, bent rims, and a missing seat, and to everyone else it was nothing but scrap. But Mike said to the owner, "How much do you want for that?"

I was shocked Mike even wanted it. But even more surprising was the ninety-seven-year-old guy living on fumes who said, "I don't think I wanna part with that."

Undeterred, Mike persisted: "How about a hundred bucks?"

The man used a wheelchair and apparently had little time left to live, but he shook his head. "I still might have use for that."

Are you kidding me? He wasn't even aware he *had* it until Mike dragged it out.

That's when I started yelling at the television. I looked at Laurie, gestured with my hands, and went on a rant: "The guy has five pole barns, eight sheds, and three houses full of stuff he hasn't seen in decades and doesn't even know he has. He's breathing through an oxygen tube attached to his wheelchair, and yet he won't take a hundred bucks for a worthless bike that'll still be sitting in the shed when he dies next week." I coaxed the man through the screen, crying, "Sell the bike! Take Mike's hundred dollars! Go enjoy the best steak dinner in town!"

But he wouldn't do it. He chose to hang on to it. And the pickers made a whole show about it.

# MINDLESS OBSESSION

I wonder what the History Channel would discover if they brought their cameras into my life and followed me around for a few months. What would they learn about what I value, what I treasure, and how I spend my time and money? What possession, hobby, habit, or odd behavior would they expose? And when other people saw my story, would they yell at the television, "What's wrong with you? Why are you pursuing that? Why are you so obsessed with that? How many fishing boots do you need?"

Everybody has healthy and positive passions in life, but how do they turn into unhealthy obsessions? When deer season arrives in November, Laurie shakes her head and says, "This is the time of year when all you little men lose your little minds." It's true. When the rut is on, it's all I can think about. For about two weeks in November, I am completely enthralled by wind direction, cold fronts, trail cameras, and scent control. To average people, my behavior could seem completely irrational, and it may make them wonder, *What happened to Pastor Bob? Has he lost his mind?*

And they would be right. I actually do lose my mind for about twelve days, and if it turned into a year-round obsession, I'd lose a lot more than that—I'd lose my marriage, job, and family too. What might *your* obsession be? Maybe it's your kids' sports, bodybuilding, NASCAR, or the perfect wine.

The definition of *obsess* is "to think about something unceasingly," and the definition of *obsession* is "the domination of one's thoughts."[1] When you're obsessed with something, you can't stop thinking about it. It determines what you do and where you go, and it becomes the driving force in your life that can blind you to other realities. While hobbies, interests, and passions are good, obsessions dangerously dominate your life and cause you to miss the new life of love, joy, and peace.

Furthermore, obsessions occupy the space in your soul that belongs to God. If these preoccupations squeeze God out, you'll carry an emptiness inside that'll never go away. It's why many people struggle with anxiety, depression, and fear. When everything else but God saturates my soul, it gets sick because it's starving for God's love.

It's taken me a lifetime to wrap my head around this, and I'm still learning. But I've discovered that nothing can satisfy me or calm my spirit if God isn't at my soul's center. If I've packed my life so full of work, golf, friends, travel, entertainment, mystery novels, and social media that every waking moment something is vying for my attention, then my soul suffers. The same is true for you. If you've filled that empty place in your soul with anything but God, then the love, joy, and peace you long for will be missing. The late, great Billy Graham said, "The soul was made for God, and without God it is restless and in secret torment."[2]

Your soul is the most important part of you. It's the part that experiences love, joy, peace, and courage, but it's also the part that experiences anxiety, loneliness, and despair. So how's the condition of your soul these days? Is it joyful or restless? At peace or in secret torment? Is it *well* with your soul?

## SOUL SICK: YEARNING FOR LESS OBSESSION, MORE DEVOTION

Doctors attend to our *physical* ailments, but where do we go when we feel sick in our spirits? What doctor can fix a weak and weary soul? What cure is there when hope is gone and we don't feel as if we can face another day? Yes, godly counselors and psychologists can be helpful, and sometimes they may be essential guides toward healing. But ultimately, only God can truly address the deepest needs of our souls.

If you've ever heard someone say, "I feel like my life's falling apart" or "I can't seem to get control of myself" or "I'm coming apart at the seams," these are the cries of a weak or wounded soul. The psalmist knew this desperation well. In Psalm 88:3 he wrote, "My soul is filled with troubles. And my life comes near the grave" (NLV). The psalmist connected the dots—because his soul was in trouble, *he* was in trouble. When his soul was sick, it actually made him physically weak and he felt as though he couldn't go on. Have you ever been so soul sick that it was difficult to exercise or do physical work? What pill is there for a troubled soul? While medicines can ease the pain for a time and sometimes have a role in healing, none of them cure a troubled soul.

The Bible teaches the connection between our bodies and souls in several places. Psalm 84:2 says, "With my whole being, *body and soul*, I will shout joyfully to the living God" (NLT). Proverbs 16:24 affirms, "Kind words are like honey—sweet to the soul and healthy for the body" (NLT). You're not just a soul, and you're not just a body. You are soul *and* body, and a healthy soul makes your entire being feel healthy.

Many of us forget to nurture our souls. We don't feed, protect, or sometimes even think about them. We don't always ask God to fill us with His love, joy, and peace. Instead, we chase our obsessions to the utter neglect of our souls. This is a problem because it's imperative to have a degree of spiritual wholeness *before* the wave hits, or it can completely overwhelm us. But we leave our souls in such a depleted and weak condition that when a rogue wave hits, we collapse into despair. "There is no zap that suddenly makes a person … whole," wrote John Eldredge. "Wholeness is something we grow into as we walk with Jesus through the years of our lives."[3]

Here's the truth: life is going to whack all of us, and when the wave hits, we can't just zap our souls into health to withstand the blow. If we fail at work, go through a breakup, get rejected by a friend, lose our health, suffer a miscarriage, face divorce, or are pulled down into despair by something weighty, we can't just flip a switch and make it all better. There's no pill we can take, movie we can watch, or thing we can order online to make us feel loved, safe, and whole.

When Horatio Spafford lost his children at sea, he strung these words into a song: "When sorrows like sea billows roll; / Whatever my lot, Thou hast taught me to say, / 'It is well, it is well with my soul.'"[4] Where did Horatio find the strength to write those words? Sorrows like sea billows will roll into our lives, and when they do, will we also be able to say, "Whatever my lot, it is well with my soul"?

## SOUL REPAIR

A few years ago Laurie and I went through what a sixteenth-century monk, Saint John of the Cross, called the "dark night" of the soul.[5] We experienced no specific tragedy or train wreck in life but rather the convergence of some challenges at work, a book deadline, interpersonal issues, and what I can describe only as an intense spiritual attack. All this hovered over us like a dark cloud.

My soul felt heavy and afraid, and I felt as if I were walking around with a bull's-eye on my chest. Laurie sensed it too, so we went to counseling and intensified our spiritual disciplines. During that time it was not well with our souls. And that reality forced us to deepen our prayer, increase our Bible reading, and spend more time in devotion to God.

Paul encouraged God's people to incorporate such disciplines: "Devote yourselves to prayer" (Col. 4:2) and "Let the peace of Christ rule in your hearts" (3:15) and "Let the message of Christ dwell among you richly" (3:16). Paul showed us how faithfulness to prayer and reading and memorizing God's Word is the pathway to peace, and Laurie and I clung to that promise. Full peace came slowly, and our need drove us to Christ in prayer continually. But I can't imagine facing that kind of darkness from a soul completely depleted because of a pattern of neglect. Had we entered that season with spiritually weak souls, we might not have survived it. Even Laurie said, "Our marriage would've survived, but I don't know if our relationship would have." Her statement pierced my heart and drove us closer to the only One who could heal our hearts and restore our hope.

Finding the new life of love, joy, and peace the Bible promises requires less obsession and more devotion. I can't possibly overstate that truth. The life we all crave cannot be found in any person, hobby, vacation home, possession, retirement fund, golf swing, or kid's sports. Those obsessions cannot do what we want them to; they can't deliver us from the old life and move us into the new. We *have* to put God at the center of our souls. Philip Yancey wrote about C. S. Lewis finding that as a Christian you do the same things you always did only with a different spirit. Lewis said, "Every single act and feeling, every experience, whether pleasant or unpleasant, must be referred to God."[6]

You don't have to give up the things you enjoy, but instead, you do them with God's daily presence and guidance. That's when life really comes alive and God begins to fill you with things you never expected or even knew about. Here's a simple way to envision it ...

Instead of thinking of this devotion like a workout, where you fit God into a time slot in your day or week, you invite Him into every part of your day. You may cultivate this habit over time, or a season of suffering can trigger it, a season when you reach the end of yourself. Regardless of how this devotion is sparked, it begins as you start asking God to walk with you all through your day—to lead you, fill you with His Spirit, protect and encourage you.

I'm a pretty resilient guy, but the other day I felt beaten down and depressed. I needed a reset. So I got on my bike and rode hard for twenty miles. As I pedaled, I prayed out loud, "Jesus, ride with me. I need You, fill me with Your Spirit, and strengthen my inner being. Put Your hand on my life and do Your restorative work while I ride." And He did. Instead of just riding my bike, I intentionally asked Jesus to cruise along with me—and it made all the difference.

The Bible describes this a few ways: "walk[ing] by the Spirit" (Gal. 5:16), "[being] led by the Spirit" (5:18), and "[being] filled by the Spirit" (Eph. 5:18). It's being aware of His presence all day long and confident of His love for you amid all the challenges you face. Sarah Young wrote, "Stay alert to the many choice-points along the way, being continually aware of My [God's] Presence. You will get through this day one way or the other. One way is to moan and groan, stumbling along [without Me].... [Or] you can choose to walk with Me along the path of Peace, leaning on Me as much as you need."[7] The psalmist David made this choice, saying, "My soul, find rest in God" (Ps. 62:5).

Honestly, I feel like a complete novice in this area of devotion. I'm not a C. S. Lewis, Sarah Young, Dallas Willard, Anne Lamott, or Saint Augustine. I'm a bald little man named Bob. I sit in tree stands, listen to Eric Church, and train my dog. But I've learned that when I rush headlong into my daily activities without placing God at the center to guide me, I get sick—soul sick with anxiety, emptiness, and loneliness. I'm not an expert, but I've stumbled on four nonnegotiables that have helped me reduce my obsessions and increase my devotion.

## TAKE CHARGE OF YOUR SPIRITUAL HEALTH

We will not accidently drift into a life devoted to God, and we will not somehow stumble into spiritual transformation. If we just go with the flow, life's current will always push us onto the banks of our obsessions and into the land of sin.

Pastor and author Brian Tome wrote, "The key to changing … is to set up as many automatic systems as you can and never compromise them."[8] That's the secret to any kind of transformation—establish as many automatic habits and structures as you can, and never deviate from them.

What are some specific habits you can implement to help feed your soul? What automatic systems can you put in place that will transform your life?

Bob was sitting in our church's lobby, waiting for service to begin. I asked him how he found our church, and he said a friend invited him to Quest 180°, our addiction recovery program. He opened up and said, "After many years of being lost, I said yes to Christ, and it's changed my whole life." Bob appeared nervous, but he wanted to thank me and our church for all we've done. He went on to tell me he's in the "training-wheel stage" of faith and recently attended our Group Link program to find a small group. Admittedly it was his first time at a Bible study.

I shook Bob's hand and told him I was so glad he found us. Then I greeted a few more people and climbed the stairs to the upper section of our auditorium to enjoy the service. (I wasn't teaching that evening.) I glanced around and saw Bob sitting alone about four rows down. I thought maybe this was a God thing, so I sat down next to him. But I think that might've ruined his whole night.

I asked, "Do you mind if I sit with you?"

He said, "Pastors kinda freak me out."

"Don't worry—they freak me out too. Is this where you sit, Bob?"

He nodded. "Yup, row BB, seat nine, every Saturday."

I smiled. "Why BB, seat nine?"

"*B*'s the first letter of my name, and nine's kind of a lucky number for me. This is my seat. God meets me here."

It was Communion night, which also made him nervous because, he said, the first two times he took Communion, he couldn't get the bread out of the little packet. (It takes a genius to open our Communion packets. Someone should do something about that.)

I reassured him, saying, "Don't worry—we'll figure it out together."

"And I don't sing the songs because I can't sing," Bob clarified.

I waved my hands. "Just do what you normally do."

Things were fine—until the offering. I mean, I get it. What could be worse than sitting next to the senior pastor as the offering comes down the row? Talk about pressure. I could feel Bob's anxiety, and I tried not to look. But I glanced over and saw that Bob already had reached for his wallet. You know what he did? He pulled out a prepared check, which meant he had planned to give whether I was there or not. I thought, *I love this guy.*

And there we sat, two Bobs in row BB, hoping that God would meet us there.

Do you have a seat where God meets you? If you're looking for Bob on a Saturday night, you'll never miss him in row BB, seat nine. Not only did he sign up for a Bible study (hard to do for an introvert), but every Wednesday night he also attends our addiction recovery program. Because you don't drift into transformation. You take charge. You build structures into your life that are automatic; you know exactly where you're going to be so God can meet you there.

## COMMIT TO DAILY DEVOTION

How can I make daily devotion not sound boring? Here's how: when the pain gets so loud and, well, painful, it's not boring anymore. When sickness, loneliness, or emptiness that nothing can fix enters your soul, then the soothing calm of God's Spirit becomes something you can't live a single day without. Jesus said, "Peace I leave with you; my peace I give you. I do not give to you as the world gives. Do not let your hearts be troubled and do not be afraid" (John 14:27).

How do we get that kind of peace? Jesus clued us in a few verses later when He said, "Remain in me, as I also remain in you. No branch can bear fruit by itself; it must remain in the vine.... I am the vine; you are the branches.... Apart from me you can do nothing" (John 15:4–5).

We're not just bodies, and we're not just souls. Each of us has a body and a soul. Every morning we feed and nurture our bodies with breakfast food and the drink of heaven: coffee. Our bodies rely on our daily intake of food. But how many of us bolt out the door and speed through our day with souls that are starving for spiritual nourishment? Not just once—but we do it for days on end? Jesus said, "Apart from me you can do nothing." A person can live without food for a few weeks, but how long can someone live with a God-starved soul? The rise of anxiety, depression, and suicide indicates we can't live for long—at least not live well.

One of the benefits of aging (there aren't many) is you don't feel like living at Mach 2 anymore. You slow down and actually welcome quiet moments, so it's easier for older people to spend a few minutes each day in prayer and in the Bible. When I was younger, it was a chore, a duty, but not anymore. I welcome it like my morning coffee, and I actually can't live without my time alone with God. My soul yearns for Him. I find when I devote a few minutes to prayer and reading the Bible, I'm like a "tree planted by streams of water, which yields its fruit in season and whose leaf does not wither" (Ps. 1:3). When I miss that time because of golf or traveling, I can tell my soul is weakened, and I don't have the strength and peace that come from being connected to the Vine. My soul finds rest in God alone. (If you need help in this area, one of the best tools available today is a Bible app. Most large churches offer them. You can access ours at eaglebrookchurch.com/app, and every day we provide a devotional paired with a Scripture passage, a Scripture memorization challenge, or another way to spend time with God. It's one of the best tools I know that can cure a hurting and tired soul. Bible Gateway and YouVersion are also great resources.)

It's time to be done with starving our souls and begin connecting to the Vine, who gives and sustains life. Remain in Him every day, and I know He'll fill spaces in your soul with things you never knew about and soon won't be able to live without.

## BATTLE THE ENEMY

We think our main problems are with a cranky coworker, a defiant child, or an injured shoulder, but Paul wrote, "Our struggle is not against flesh and blood, but against the rulers, against the authorities, against the powers of this dark world and against the spiritual forces of evil in the heavenly realms" (Eph. 6:12). As much as we think our fight is against things we can see, we must turn our eyes to a different reality. How many of us are actually aware Satan is working day and night to destroy our souls and lives? How often do we realize that spiritual forces are looking for opportunities to assault us? "Then war broke out in heaven. Michael and his angels fought against the dragon, and the dragon and his angels fought back. But he was not strong enough, and they lost their place in heaven. The great dragon was hurled down—that ancient serpent called the devil, or Satan, who leads the whole world astray.... Woe to the earth and the sea, because the devil has gone down to you! He is filled with fury, because he knows that his time is short" (Rev. 12:7–9, 12).

Satan and his demons are loose on earth, and they have power to destroy. But every Christian actually holds the authority and power to defeat them. And it's not just a future victory; the victory has already happened. Satan and his foul spirits were already defeated—past tense. When Jesus was crucified and rose from the dead, He broke the curse of sin and death, and "having disarmed the powers and authorities, he made a public spectacle of them, triumphing over them by the cross" (Col. 2:15). After His resurrection, Jesus declared, "All authority in heaven and on earth has been given to me" (Matt. 28:18).

Let that sink in. *All authority* in the *heavens* and *all authority* on this *planet* has been given to Jesus Christ. And what's more—don't miss this—He's passed along His authority to *us*: "I have given you authority ... to overcome all the power of the enemy" (Luke 10:19).

In His power Jesus has given us armor and a weapon to use. "Stand firm [against Satan] then, with the belt of truth" (Eph. 6:14). Read God's Word, memorize its promises, and use this book of ultimate truth against the Enemy, who is "a liar and the father of lies" (John 8:44). The Bible clearly states that you are beloved by God, chosen, adopted, protected, and called. Don't let Satan cause you to believe otherwise.

We also have a "breastplate of righteousness" (Eph. 6:14). If you live rightly, you're protected from Satan's attacks. If you live wrongly, you make an opening in your armor accessible to him, and he'll use it against you and your loved ones. Cover your vital areas with righteous living so Satan can't hurt you.

"Take up the shield of faith, with which you can extinguish all the flaming arrows of the evil one" (v. 16). Did you know that Satan and his foul spirits are shooting arrows at you? You're a walking bull's-eye—so are your kids and Christian friends. But faith is your shield of protection. It seems like such a simple thing, but the Bible is precise. Our faith can block every arrow shot at us. If your faith is weak or wavering, get back to church, get back to the Bible, and surround yourself with other mature Christians who can encourage your faith and reaffirm what you believe.

"Take the helmet of salvation and the sword of the Spirit, which is the word of God. And pray in the Spirit on all occasions with all kinds of prayers and requests" (vv. 17–18). You have a helmet and sword. Wear them and use them every day.

"Put on the full armor of God, so that you can take your stand against the devil's schemes" (v. 11). We don't have to live in fear of our enemy, because not only do we wield authority over him but the armor and weapon to defeat him are also at our disposal. Are we using them? Or are we leaving ourselves, our family, our friends, and everyone else we care about wide open to spiritual attack and defeat?

Be done with that. Refuse to live unprotected any longer. Pick up the resources Christ has given you and strap on faith.

My wife and I pray against Satan's attacks every day, and I urge you to do the same. Our prayer goes something like this:

> Jesus, all authority in heaven and on earth has been given to You and, in turn, given to us. Thank You for defeating the Evil One and giving us victory over him and his foul spirits too. Right now we claim Your authority over our enemy, and in Your name we ask You to destroy him. Bind him from hurting or attacking our marriage, kids, grandkids, staff, and church in any way. In faith we claim Your promise to protect us from his fiery arrows. Your kingdom come; Your will be done on earth even as it is in heaven. And deliver us from the Evil

One—for Yours is the power, kingdom, and glory forever. Amen.

## FIND GOD IN THE STILLNESS

"Be still, and know that I am God" (Ps. 46:10). *To be still* means "to be still." This seems obvious, but it begs repeating. We must pause our moving, running, planning, and scurrying about to *know* God.

The Hebrew word translated *know* has a sense of intimacy and oneness. In our stillness we become aware it's no longer us against the world. God is with us, and when we acknowledge and surrender to His sovereignty, no matter our circumstances, we're declaring in that space and quietude, "God, You got this."

Twenty years ago I read a statement from John Ortberg that's done more for my spiritual growth than any other. John shared about a time when he felt the need for advice about the pace of his life and the condition of his heart. So he called his mentor, Dallas Willard, for help and asked what he should do to be healthy spiritually. John said there was a long pause on the phone before the wise theologian spoke. Finally Dallas said calmly, "You must ruthlessly eliminate hurry from your life."

After another long pause John said, "Okay, I've written that one down. That's a good one. Now what else is there?" He had lots to do, so John wanted to get as much wisdom out of this call as possible.

Another long pause. Then Dallas replied, "There is nothing else. You must ruthlessly eliminate hurry from your life."

Hurry was so normal for John he didn't even realize he was doing it right then: "Ruthlessly eliminate hurry. Okay, what else you got—and hurry up about it."[9]

Ortberg noted that many of us suffer from what's called *hurry sickness*. We collect *major purchases* that add hurry to our lives, like a boat, cabin, or motorcycle—because now we have to maintain them, use them, and store them. *People* accelerate time. Some of us carry too many friendships, and they keep us running from one commitment to another. *Traveling* speeds up life. You race to catch your flight, live out of a suitcase, and scramble from point A to point B. *Kids* fast-forward time unlike anything else. You blink once, and suddenly they're no longer in diapers and you're moving them into college. *Moving to a new place.* Because now you have to update, cancel, and change things ... and find new dentists, new schools, new friends, and a new church.

Be done with unnecessary additions to your life in an effort to ruthlessly eliminate hurry. Our souls will not find rest if we're caught up in the hustle and racing from place to place to drop off our kids at their activities, meet a client over dinner, and make a Target run in between. Rather, God is found and souls are restored in the stillness. As David said, "He leads me beside quiet waters, he refreshes my soul" (Ps. 23:2–3).

Four years ago my soul was dangerously depleted. I'd just come out of the intensive eight-month-long evaluation of my leadership I told you about, which included 125 pages of feedback—all very personal and emotional. I was dealing with the recent loss of a very close friend whose funeral I had to officiate. And my heart hadn't totally healed from a hard ministry year that included difficult staff transitions. I knew I needed an extended time of solitude for God to do His loving repair work.

Fortunately, I had planned a kind of "bucket list" bow-hunting trip that fall, and nothing slows my rpms better than a few days in the woods with my bow. So right after services one Sunday, I left for Montana with a close friend and a dangerously exhausted soul. By the next morning I was so far off the grid in elk country that I felt transported to another world. My friend Ron guided me for three days up and down mountain ravines, across ice-cold trout streams, and through dense forest.

We didn't see or hear any elk for three days, but on the fourth morning, Ron let out a bugle before daylight and a bull answered from about a half mile away. For the next thirty minutes, Ron called and the bull answered across the valley and timber.

Ron moved quickly and set up thirty yards behind me. "He's coming hard," Ron asserted. "Hide behind those trees, and I'll keep calling." I started to hyperventilate, my glasses fogged up, I got down on my knees, and my whole body shook. And then this massive creature appeared. Coming right toward me, a hundred yards away through the timber, was an six-hundred-pound bull elk. Steam blew from his nostrils, and my heart pounded out of my chest. He was looking for a girlfriend when suddenly he stopped twenty yards away and stared me down. He was a younger bull, and the shot wasn't right. So I lowered my bow and allowed him to pass. As quickly as he charged into my life, he trotted off and disappeared.

I fell backward onto the soft pine needles and mountain laurel with my arms outstretched toward heaven in total awe of what had just happened. I still remember that moment, the stillness of the air and the close encounter with that wild and glorious animal. And I wish a thousand times over that I could bask in God's presence on that bed of pine needles again.

By the time I sat up on the forest floor that crisp morning, shards of sunlight streamed through the mountain timber, and I noticed a little spark of joy and gratitude flicker deep down in my soul. I hadn't felt that in weeks.

The next day Ron and another friend went fly-fishing on the Blackfoot River. Imagine fly-fishing in Montana on the Blackfoot, where the movie *A River Runs through It* was set. But you know what I did? I passed! I stayed behind because I knew I needed more time alone to recover—more of that space and quiet I experienced the previous day. It was one of the best days of my life, and I knew it was God's gift. That glorious day I read Ruth Haley Barton's *Strengthening the Soul of Your Leadership*, and God used it prophetically. I journaled my thoughts, took two naps, went for a walk, lay on the couch, and stared at the mountains.

But mostly I was alone with God, and I asked Him to heal me, to restore and strengthen me by His Spirit. In my prayer time I asked Him to fill me with every good thing He has for me. And during my Bible reading, I asked Him to speak to me. Because it's not just about being alone—you have to intentionally invite God into your disciplines of devotion.

Truly it was one of the best days I've had in many years. God led me beside quiet waters, He restored my soul, and He filled my empty spaces with things I never knew about—a new kind of love, a new kind of joy, and new kinds of peace that the world and all its obsessions can never supply.

## DISCUSSION QUESTIONS

1. We often try to fit God into part of our day or week. But what would it look like for you to invite Him into every part of your day?

2. What are some automatic systems you can implement to feed your soul and transform your life? *Get to church every week*

3. Read 2 Corinthians 5:17. What are you done with in the old life? The old has gone; the new has come—how are you walking into new life today? Praise Jesus for making a way, giving us a new start, and freeing your soul forevermore.

CONCLUSION

# GONE FOR GOOD

Jason Strand, our teaching pastor, and his wife, Sarah, already had three sons and a daughter, so when he told me they were expecting baby number five, I blurted out, "Are you kidding?" And then I realized that wasn't the best response and backtracked. "I mean, congratulations. But seriously … what were you thinking?"

Jason's second son, Hudson, loves life and turns everything into an adventure—even bath time. As a five-year-old, Hudson donned snorkel gear and spent most bath times facedown in the tub, searching for things. Even when it was time to get out, Hudson took one look up at his parents and dove back under five inches of water with goggles on. Jason would ask, "What are you doing under there? What are you looking at as you skim the surface of our tub?" There were no fish, no sea creatures, and no rock formations, but every time Hudson bathed, on went the goggles and down he dove.

Last March Jason's family traveled down to Orlando, Florida. They headed straight to a number of swimming pools, but what caught their attention was an enormous saltwater pool nearby. It was thirty to forty feet deep and filled with all sorts of saltwater life. From a distance it looked like all the other pools, but inside were stingrays, sharks, exotic fish of all colors and shapes, and multicolored coral with sea urchins. Everyone was amazed.

Of course, Hudson dove in first. With his goggles and breathing tube strapped on, he swam facedown across the surface in this aquatic paradise. Thirty seconds later, he popped up, threw off his mask, and yelled, "Mom, Dad, this is awesome! I just swam over a stingray!" For a kid who'd snorkeled in the bathtub all his life, this was the best moment of his life.

As Jason told this story to our church, he paused, looked into the eyes of our congregation, and asked, "I wonder how many of us have been snorkeling in the bathtub all our lives?"

## RESTORE YOUR WOW

Psalm 19:1 says, "The heavens declare the glory of God; the skies proclaim the work of his hands."

Every day the earth rotates at just the right speed to cause the sun to shine through our bedroom windows every morning. The realization that this enormous world is suspended in space without any cables or structures holding it in place and no machine causing it to spin is mind boggling. We should absolutely be in awe that our earth spins at approximately 1,000 miles per hour and orbits the sun at about 67,000 miles per hour.

Question: Why does it spin? No reason. Except that God made it spin. Our planet also orbits the sun at just the right angle so we don't freeze or burn. And the moon is just the right size and distance to stabilize the earth's tilt and keep the tides working precisely for life to exist. Even small variations in the precision of those things would cause such dramatic swings in climate and gravity that life on earth would be nearly intolerable, if not impossible.

Then God created you and me. Think of it. I love the detail in Psalm 139:13–14: "You knit me together in my mother's womb.... I am fearfully and wonderfully made." Do you believe that about yourself? You are no accident; God had you in mind before you were even born. Ask people who knit, and they'll explain they start with a plan and then form every stitch, every little detail, according to the plan. God says, "You are wonderfully made, and I knit you together just how I wanted you to be."

Science can explain *how* one microscopic sperm out of one hundred million unites with an egg, which then becomes a living, breathing, thinking, talking human being. Yet the creation of life involves mysteries that science cannot explain. This tiny cell contains the entire DNA determining a person's height, hair, eye color, intelligence, drive, and personality, and that cell then becomes Bob Merritt, Bubba Watson, or Carrie Underwood—uniquely designed with a specific personality and purpose in life.

Does it ever wow you that out of your father's millions of sperm, the one that had your name on it found the egg and your unique life began? And to know that God planned you to be uniquely you?

As if that weren't enough, God says, "I love you. More than anything else. I desire to have a relationship with you, and I want to help you escape the old life of anxiety, fear, sin, and death. I want to show you a new life of love, joy, peace, and eternal life. I want you to leave the bathtub and be done with that for good. I want you to swim freely in the ocean of My love and never look back."

It's there.

It's yours.

Are you ready to be done with the deadness of your old life? Done with the stranglehold of your signature sins? Done with the middle and the misery of living in both worlds?

Are you ready to fight against rebellion and uphold obedience? Have less and give more? Take your eyes off yourself and turn them more toward others? Become less obsessed, more devoted?

Are you done with that?

## A FINAL PROMISE

Clearly I love my dog, but Blue's taken up a nasty habit and, about once a year, runs away. This last time, I was looking forward to dinner and a quiet evening with Laurie. I whistled out our back door for Blue to come inside. But there was no sign of him. It was dark, frigid, ten-degree weather, and I was exhausted and in no mood for his antics. But I bundled up—hat, boots, and a head lamp—and trekked through the back woods and into the enormous frozen cattail swamp bordering our property. I found his tracks in the snow and followed them into the swamp as far as I could.

But then I lost him when his tracks intersected those of coyotes.

I came back home, then drove all over the neighborhood, yelling and whistling for him. But it was hopeless. These were my exact words to Laurie: "I'm done. He might die out there tonight, but there's nothing I can do. *I've had it with him.*"

Laurie sat quietly, and I knew she wouldn't sleep. I knew she had a knot in her stomach. Finally she said, "Let's drive around one more time."

But I shook my head and said, "Laur, I've had it. If you want to go and give it one last try, go ahead." So she did. And she prayed a simple prayer: "Lord, guide me to our dog so I can bring him home." Nothing profound, just a small plea for God's help.

Everything was dark. Nobody was out in the neighborhood. But about a mile from home, she glimpsed a dark animal heading toward the back of someone's house. She stopped the car, took a chance, and called out his name. "Come, Blue! Come here, boy."

And Blue bounded to the car, happy as could be. Laurie said, "In that moment all I felt was gratitude to God. Ultimately, losing a dog's not a huge thing compared to other problems, but I felt God's mercy and answer to a simple prayer."

I'd given up on Blue because that's what we humans do. We get exhausted and feel defeated, so we give up, even on one another. But I want you to know more than anything that God will *never* give up on you. He's in constant pursuit of you, calling your name.

That's hard for some of you to believe because your human experience has been just the opposite. *People* gave up on you. Maybe it was a parent, sibling, spouse, friend, or teammate, and you still remember that pain well. Why would God be any different?

Because God isn't other people, and we glimpse His loving heart whenever someone lives in his or her new life. I gave up on Blue, but Laurie didn't. She went out again to look for him. Maybe some of you need to know that no matter how far or how many times you've run from God, no matter how many times you've failed or lost your way, God will *never give up on you*. God is constantly looking for you, calling your name, and hoping you'll hear His voice and let Him lead you back to a life of safety, bounty, and love. Will you let Him?

This world will always have temptation and sin, and you and I will sometimes run off and lose our way. When we do, we become vulnerable to falling back into the old patterns of darkness, danger, and fear.

When that happens, I hope you hear God saying, "You're My boy. You're My girl. Come back home. Don't look back."

The old life is gone.

A new life has come.

# NOTES

## CHAPTER 1

1. Brant Hansen, *Unoffendable: How Just One Change Can Make All of Life Better* (Nashville: W Publishing, 2015), 60.

2. Dallas Willard, *The Spirit of Disciplines: Understanding How God Changes Lives* (New York: HarperCollins, 1991), 258.

3. Willard, *Spirit of Disciplines*, 1.

## CHAPTER 2

1. Cindy Wooden, "Jesus' Love Changes People, Enables Them to Love Others, Pope Says," Catholic News Service, September 21, 2015, www.catholicnews .com/services/englishnews/2015/jesus-love-changes-people-enables-them-to -love-others-pope-says.cfm.

2. C. S. Lewis, *Mere Christianity* (New York: HarperOne, 2001), 93, emphasis added.

## CHAPTER 3

1. C. J. Mahaney, *Humility: True Greatness* (Colorado Springs: Multnomah Books, 2005), 33–34.

2. John Eldredge, *Wild at Heart: Discovering the Secret of a Man's Soul*, rev. ed. (Nashville: Thomas Nelson, 2001), 69–75.

3. Cameron Morfit, "Jason Day's Greatest Save: The GOLF Magazine Interview," *Golf*, October 9, 2015, www.golf.com/tour-and-news/jason-days-greatest-save -golf-magazine-interview; Karen Crouse, "Jason Day's Long Rise to No. 1 Began with a Mother's Save," *The New York Times*, April 5, 2016, www .nytimes.com/2016/04/06/sports/golf/jason-day-masters.html.

## CHAPTER 4

1. Henry Cloud, *Integrity: The Courage to Meet the Demands of Reality* (New York: Collins, 2006), 106–107, 109.

2. John C. Maxwell, *Intentional Living: Choosing a Life That Matters* (New York: Center Street, 2015), 13–14.

3. Maxwell, *Intentional Living*, 47–48.

4. Phil McGraw, *Family First: Your Step-by-Step Plan for Creating a Phenomenal Family* (New York: Free Press, 2004), 16.

5. McGraw, *Family First*, 17.

## CHAPTER 5

1. Chip Gaines and Joanna Gaines, *The Magnolia Story* (Nashville: W Publishing, 2016), 144–45.

2. David Brooks, *The Road to Character* (New York: Random House, 2015), 204.

3. Brooks, *The Road to Character*, 199.

## CHAPTER 6

1. Tim LaHaye, *How to Win over Depression*, rev. ed. (Grand Rapids, MI: Zondervan, 1996), 129.

2. Tim LaHaye and David Noebel, *Mind Siege: The Battle for Truth in the New Millennium* (Nashville: Word Publishing, 2000), 45–46, emphasis added.

3. "Ralph Waldo Emerson," Brainyquote.com, accessed March 2, 2019, www.brainyquote.com/quotes/ralph_waldo_emerson_108797.

4. "Marcus Aurelius," AZQuotes, accessed March 2, 2019, www.azquotes.com/quote/539017.

5. Kyle Idleman, *Gods at War: Defeating the Idols That Battle for Your Heart*, rev. ed. (Grand Rapids, MI: Zondervan, 2018), 113.

6. John Ortberg, *The Me I Want to Be: Becoming God's Best Version of You* (Grand Rapids, MI: Zondervan, 2010), 45.

7. Craig Groeschel, *Daily Power: 365 Days of Fuel for Your Soul* (Grand Rapids, MI: Zondervan, 2017), May 7.

8. David Brooks, *The Road to Character* (New York: Random House, 2015), 207.

## CHAPTER 7

1. Henry Cloud, *Necessary Endings: The Employees, Businesses, and Relationships That All of Us Have to Give Up in Order to Move Forward* (New York: Harper Business, 2010), 175–76.

2. Jacob, personal letter to author, n.d.

3. Charles R. Swindoll, *Living above the Level of Mediocrity: A Commitment to Excellence* (Nashville: W Publishing, 1989), 236–37.

## CHAPTER 8

1. Sara Merritt, conversation with author, July 20, 2017.

## CHAPTER 9

1. Sarah Young, *Jesus Calling: Enjoying Peace in His Presence* (Nashville: Thomas Nelson, 2004), 97.

## CHAPTER 10

1. Brant Hansen, *Unoffendable: How Just One Change Can Make All of Life Better* (Nashville: W Publishing, 2015), 114.

2. "Actuarial Life Table," Social Security, 2015, www.ssa.gov/OACT/STATS/table 4c6.html.

3. Erwin Raphael McManus, *Uprising: A Revolution of the Soul* (Nashville: Thomas Nelson, 2003), 140.

4. McManus, *Uprising*, 146.

5. McManus, *Uprising*, 148–49.

6. John Ortberg, *I'd Like You More if You Were More Like Me: Getting Real about Getting Close* (Carol Stream, IL: Tyndale, 2017), 242.

7. Shauna Niequist, *Present over Perfect: Leaving Behind Frantic for a Simpler, More Soulful Way of Living* (Grand Rapids, MI: Zondervan, 2016), 231–32.

8. John Eldredge, *Wild at Heart: Discovering the Secret of a Man's Soul*, rev. ed. (Nashville: Thomas Nelson, 2001), 69–71.

## CHAPTER 11

1. "Word of the Year 2013," Oxford Dictionaries, accessed March 2, 2019, https://en.oxforddictionaries.com/word-of-the-year/word-of-the-year-2013.

2. Helena Horton, "More People Have Died by Taking Selfies This Year Than by Shark Attacks," *Telegraph*, September 22, 2015, www.telegraph.co.uk /technology/11881900/More-people-have-died-by-taking-selfies-this-year -than-by-shark-attacks.html.

3. Maria Mercedes Galuppo, "Millennials Expected to Take over 25,000 Selfies in Their Lifetime," Aol.com, May 19, 2017, www.aol.com/article/news/2017 /05/19/millennials-expected-to-take-over-25-000-selfies-in-their-lifeti /22099995/.

4. Galuppo, "Millennials."

5. David Foster Wallace, *This Is Water: Some Thoughts, Delivered on a Significant Occasion, about Living a Compassionate Life* (New York: Little, Brown, 2009), 36, 39–40.

6. Kyle Idleman, *The End of Me: Where Real Life in the Upside-Down Ways of Jesus Begins* (Colorado Springs: David C Cook, 2015), 193.

7. Idleman, *End of Me*, 204.

8. John Eldredge, *Moving Mountains: Praying with Passion, Confidence, and Authority* (Nashville: Nelson Books, 2016), 1.

9. Eldredge, *Moving Mountains*, 228.

10. Judith Viorst, "If I Were in Charge of the World," in *If I Were in Charge of the World and Other Worries* (New York: Aladdin Paperbacks, 1981), 3.

## CHAPTER 12

1. *Random House Webster's Dictionary*, 4th ed. (New York: Ballantine Books, 2001), 497, s.vv. "obsess," "obsession."

2. Billy Graham, *The Secret of Happiness* (Nashville: Thomas Nelson, 2002), 19.

3. John Eldredge, *Moving Mountains: Praying with Passion, Confidence, and Authority* (Nashville: Nelson Books, 2016), 201.

4. Horatio G. Spafford, "It Is Well with My Soul," 1873, public domain.

5. Saint John of the Cross, *Dark Night of the Soul*, trans. E. Allison Peers (Mineola, NY: Dover, 2003), 1.

6. C. S. Lewis, as quoted in Philip Yancey, *Reaching for the Invisible God: What Can We Expect to Find?* (Grand Rapids, MI: Zondervan, 2000), 181.

7. Sarah Young, *Jesus Calling: Enjoying Peace in His Presence* (Nashville: Thomas Nelson, 2004), 171.

8. Brian Tome, *Free Book* (Nashville: Thomas Nelson, 2010), 140.

9. John Ortberg, *The Life You've Always Wanted: Spiritual Disciplines for Ordinary People*, rev. ed. (Grand Rapids, MI: Zondervan, 2002), 76–77.

# Get Wise